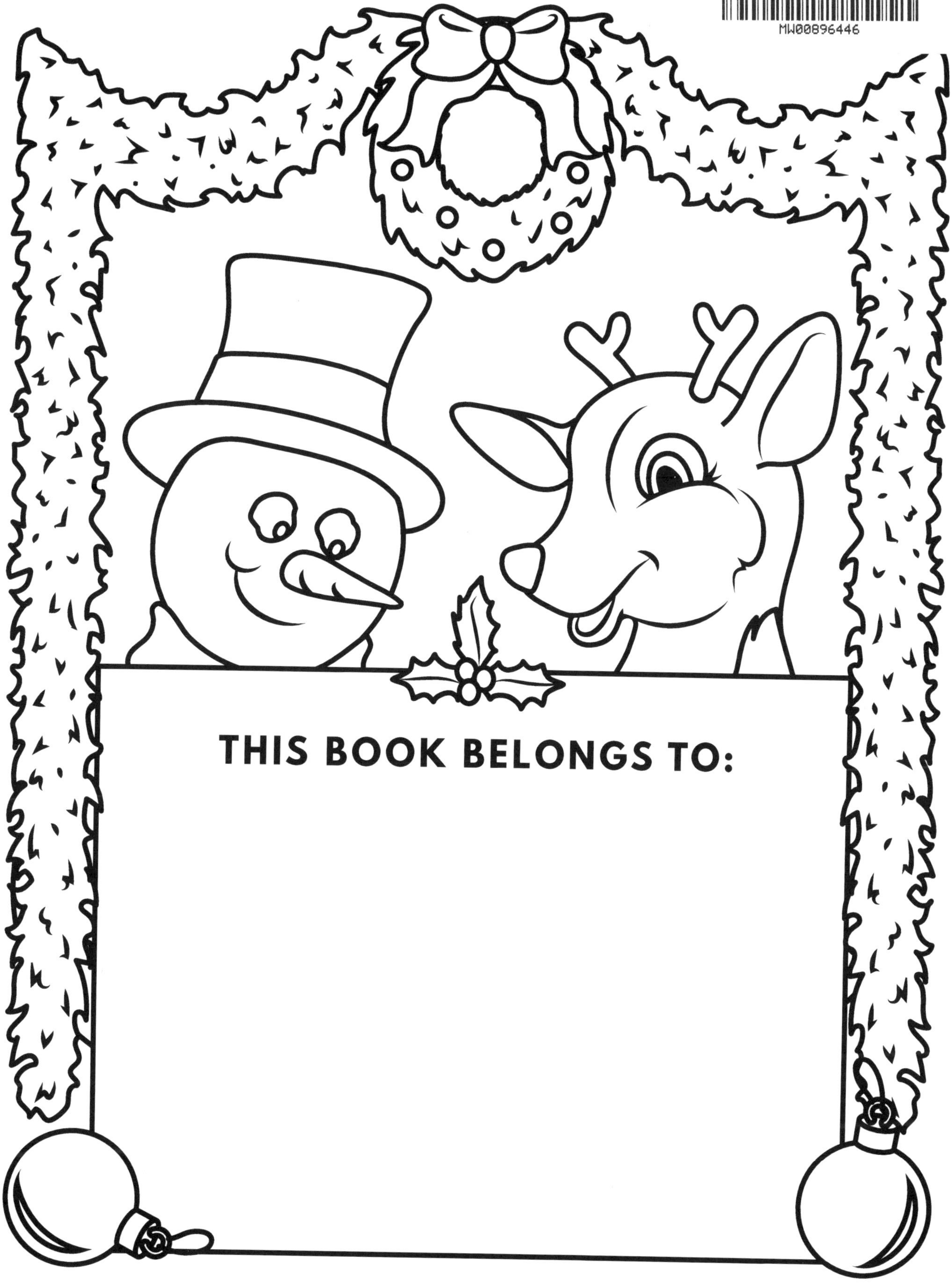
THIS BOOK BELONGS TO:

Golden Age Press

VISIT US ONLINE:
WWW.GOLDENAGEPRESS.COM

ISBN-13 : 978-1955421218

Illustrated by Roslen Roy Mack

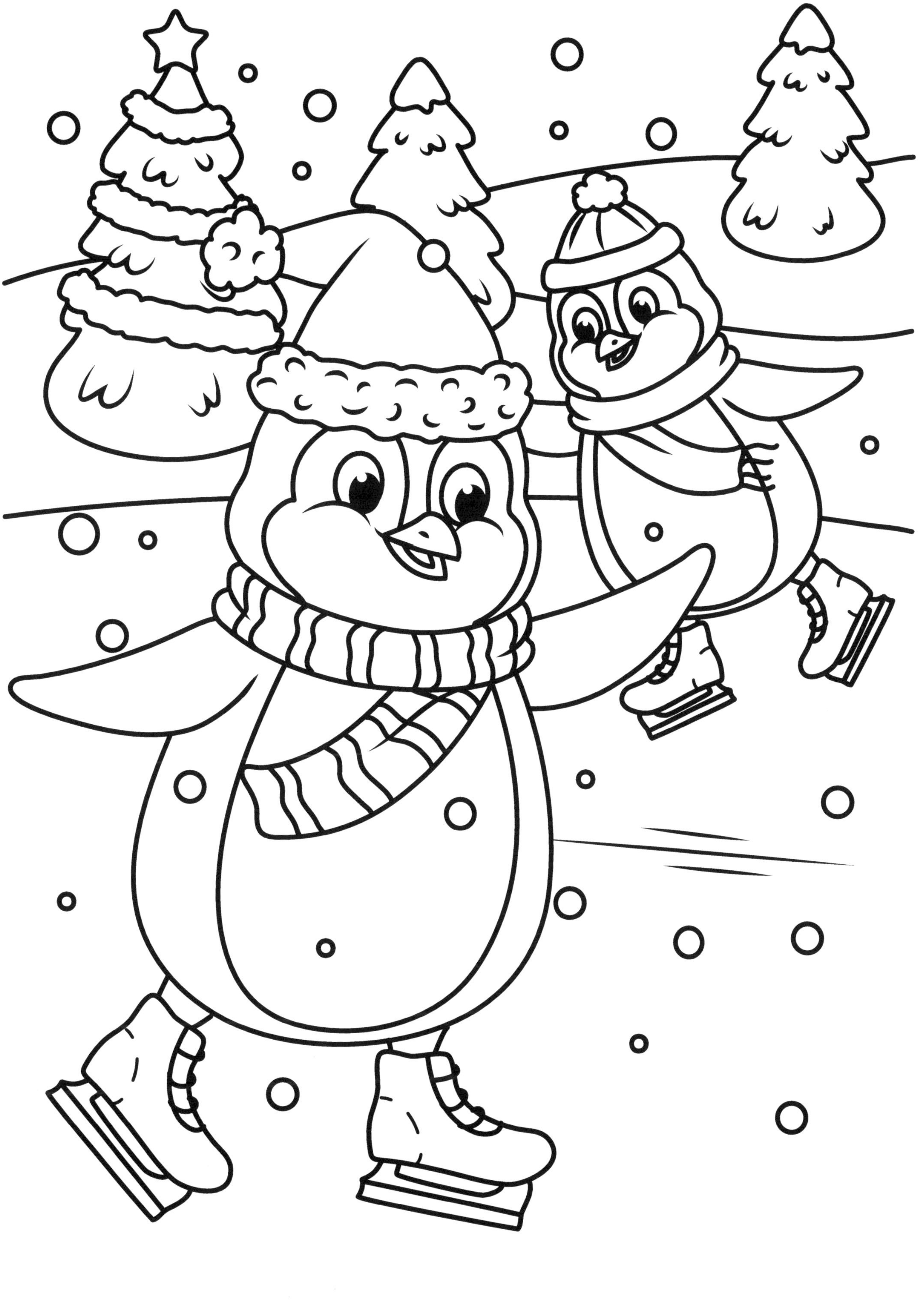

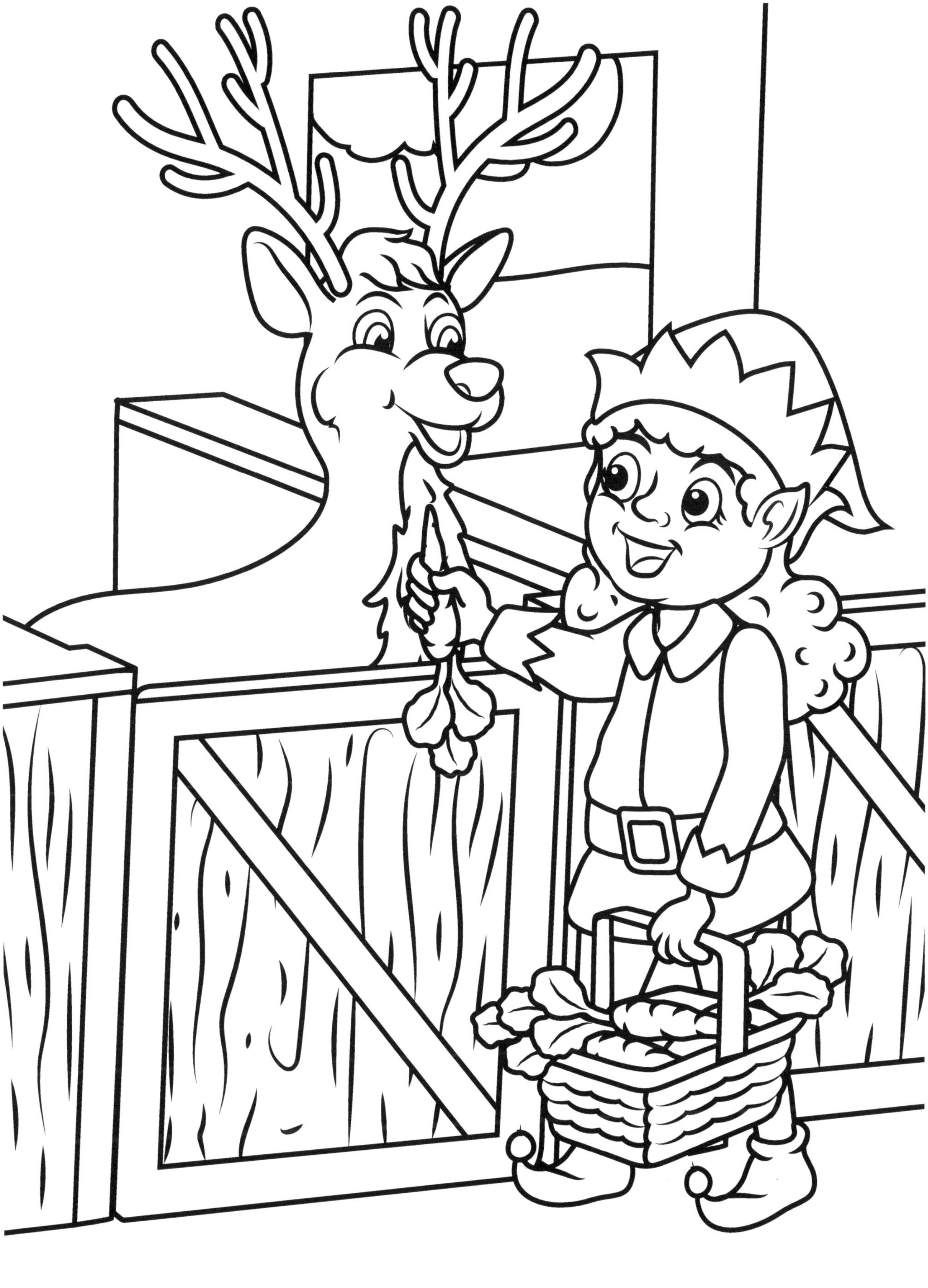

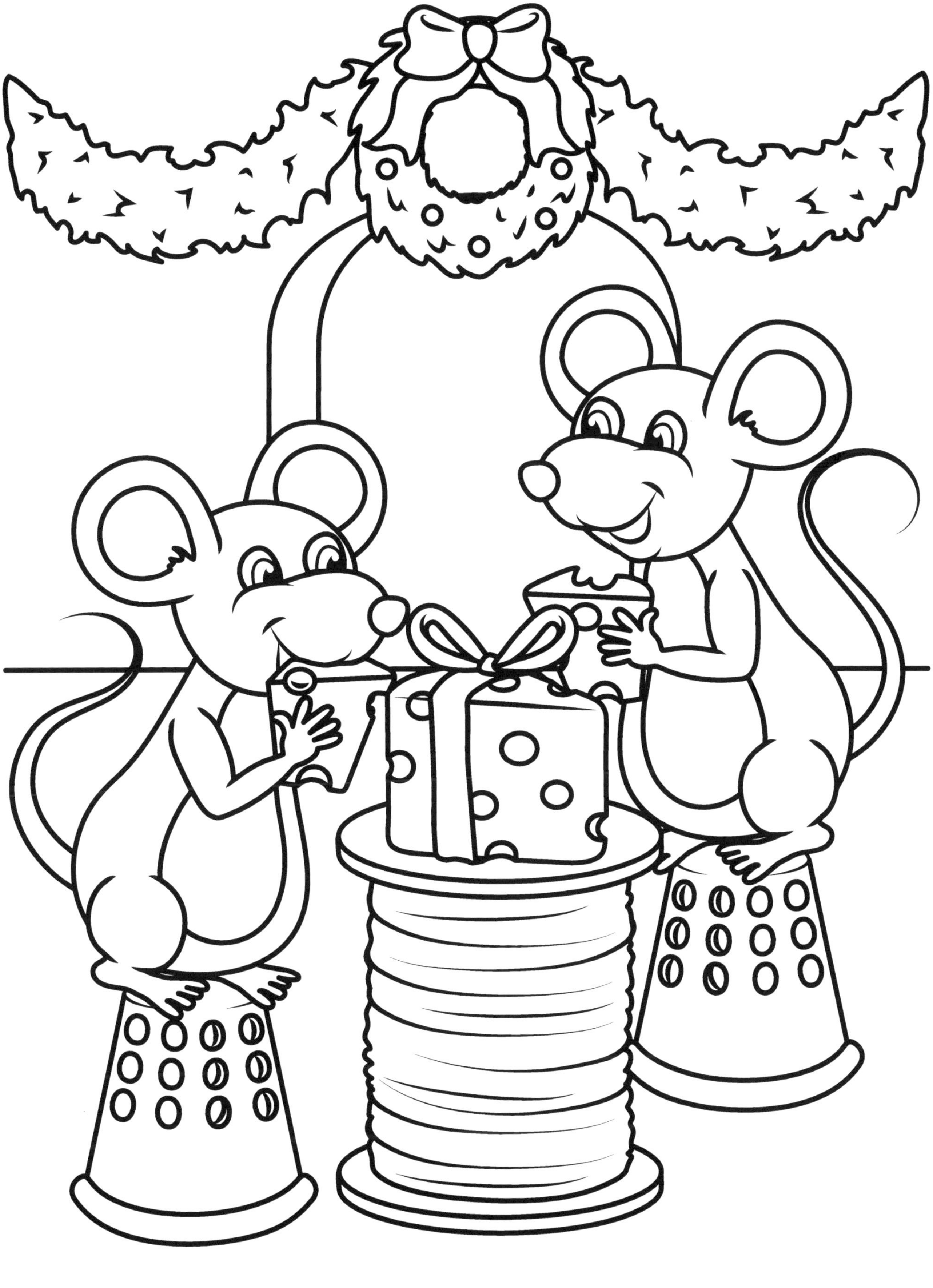

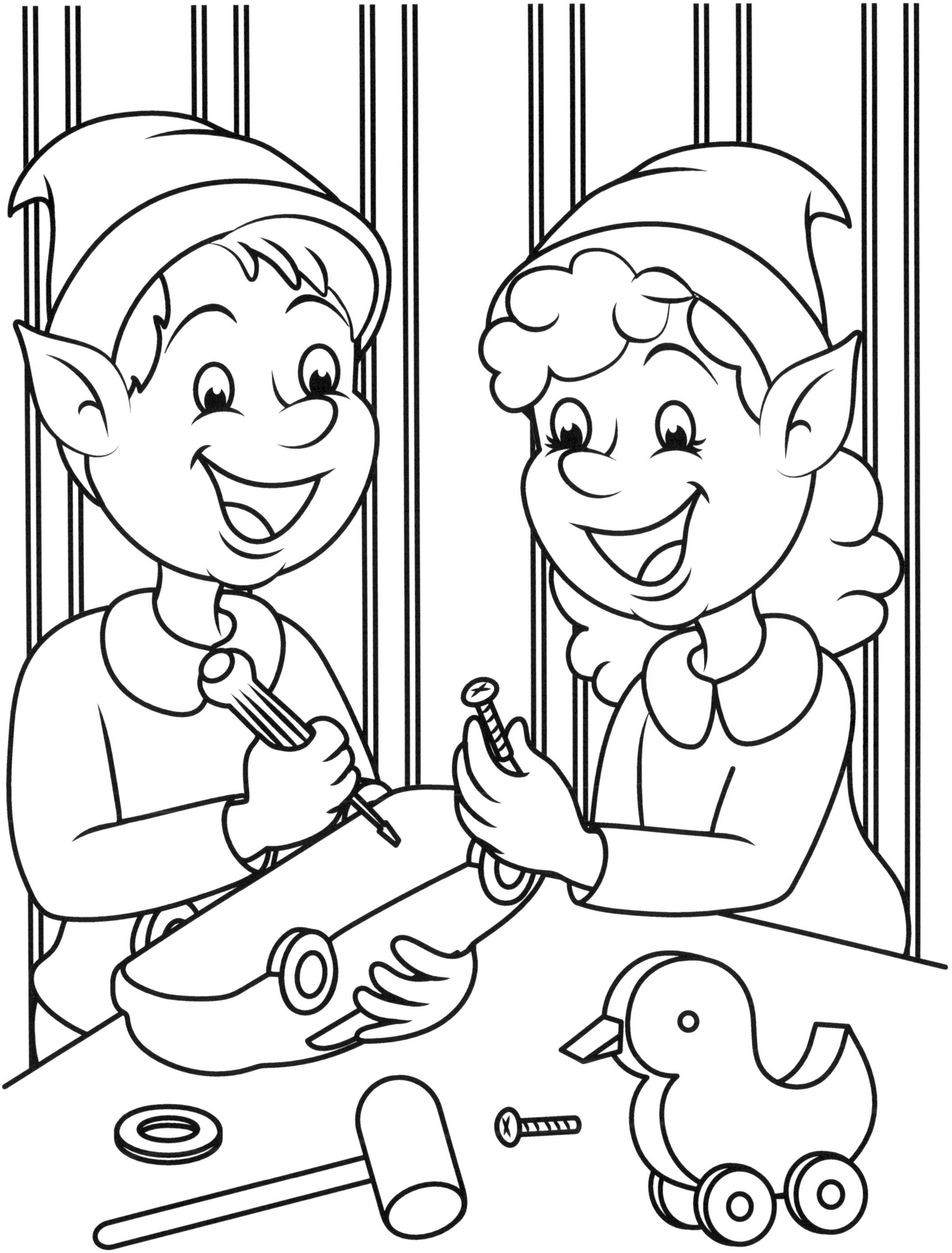

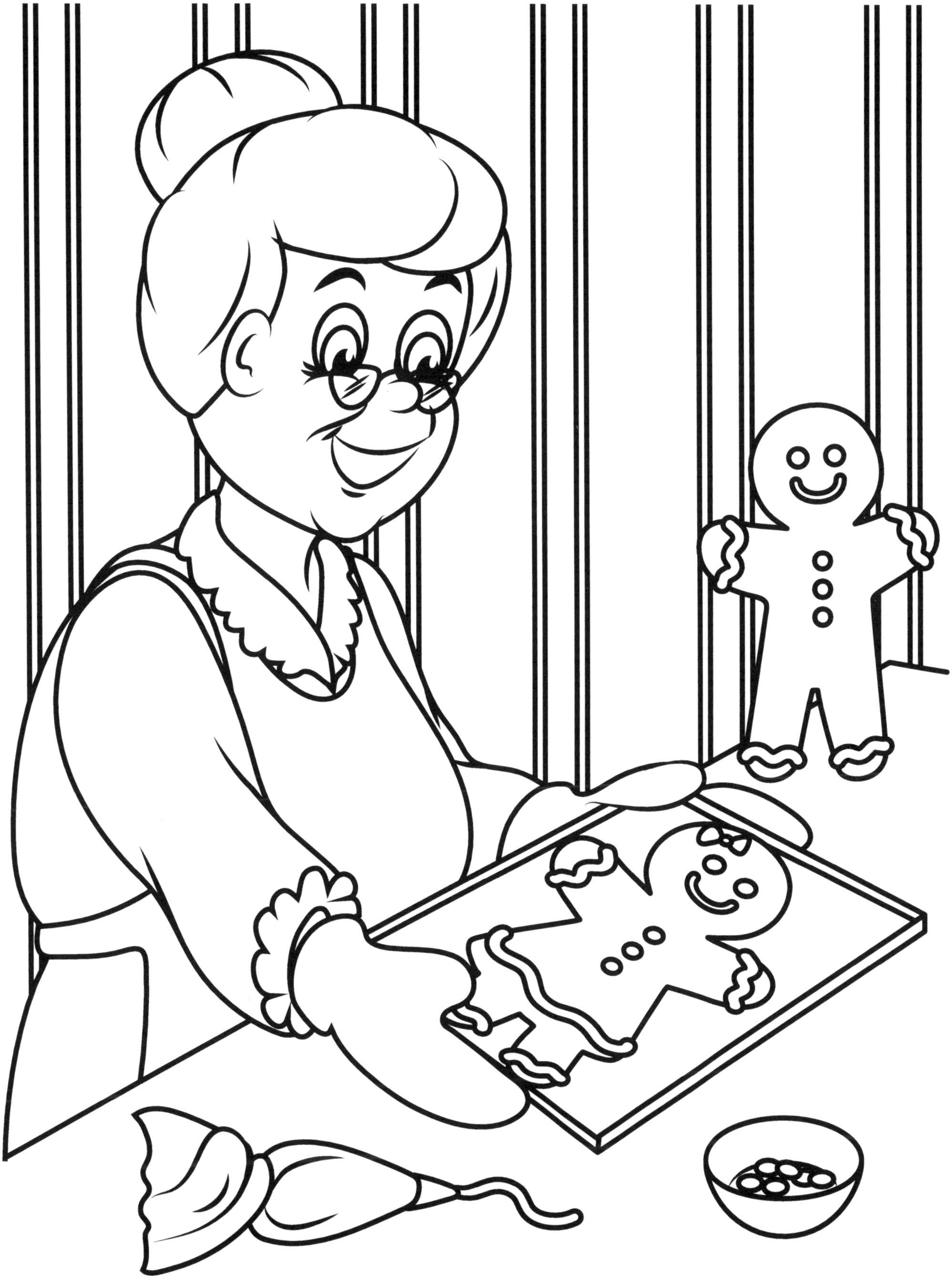

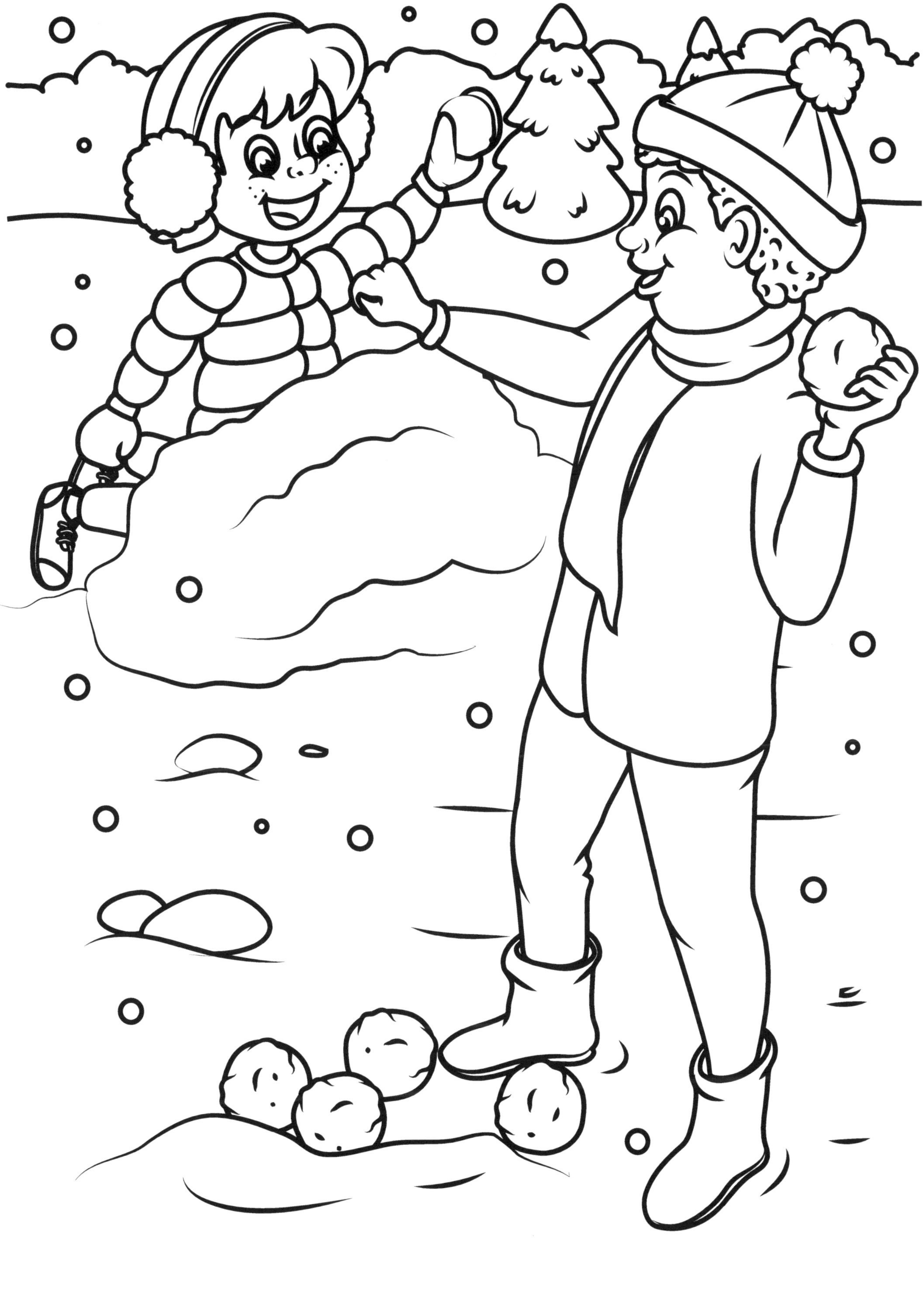

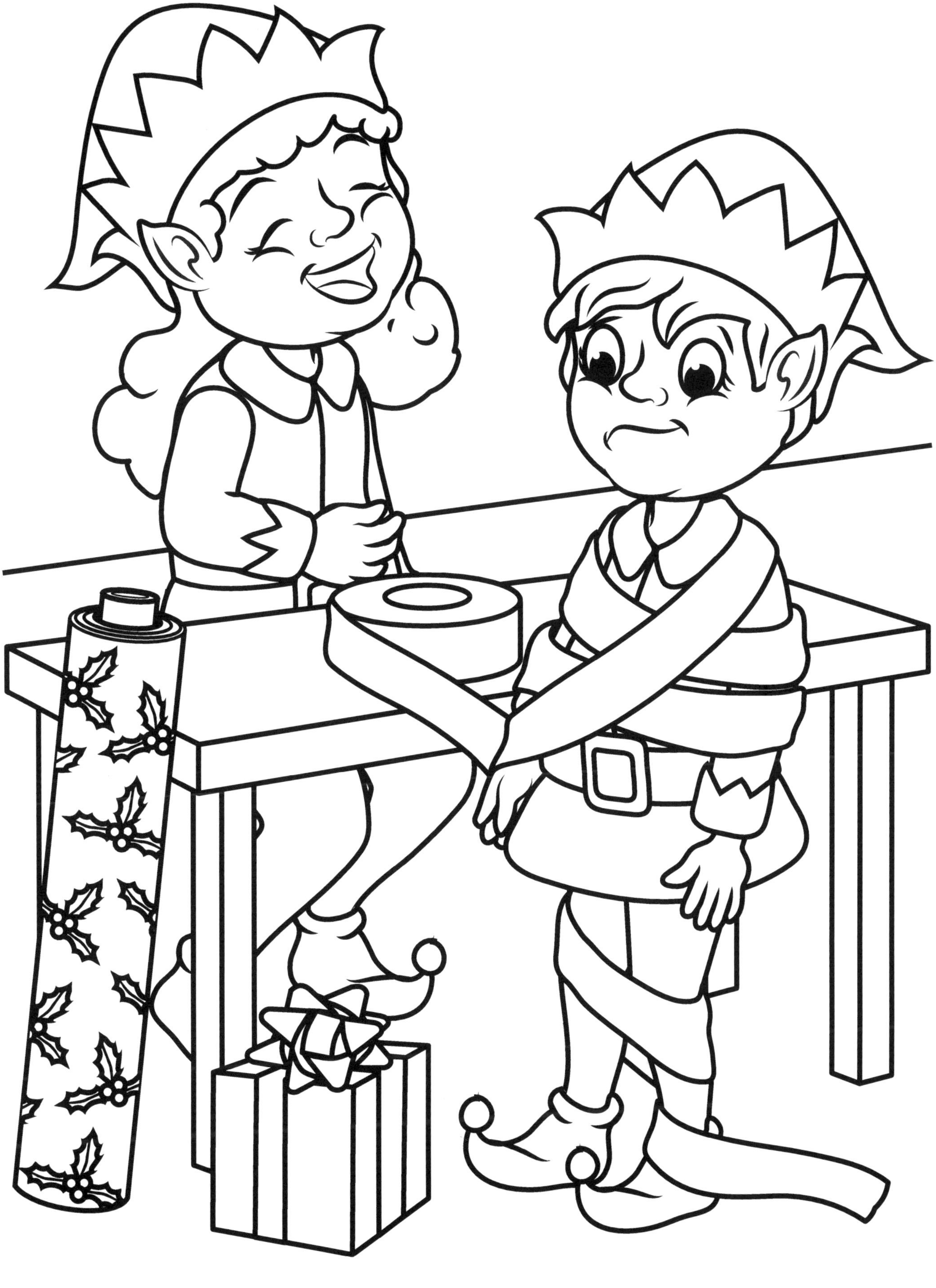

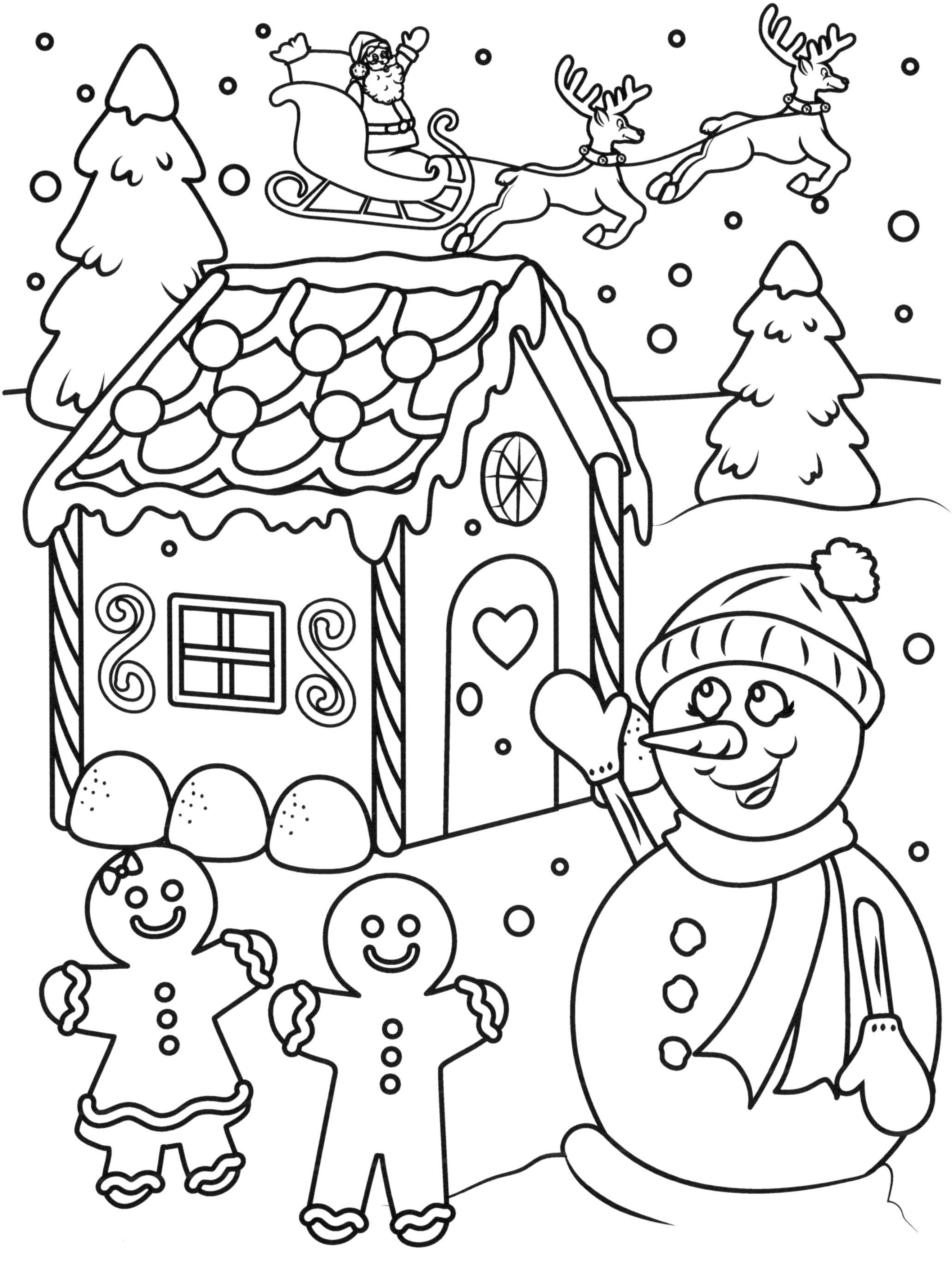

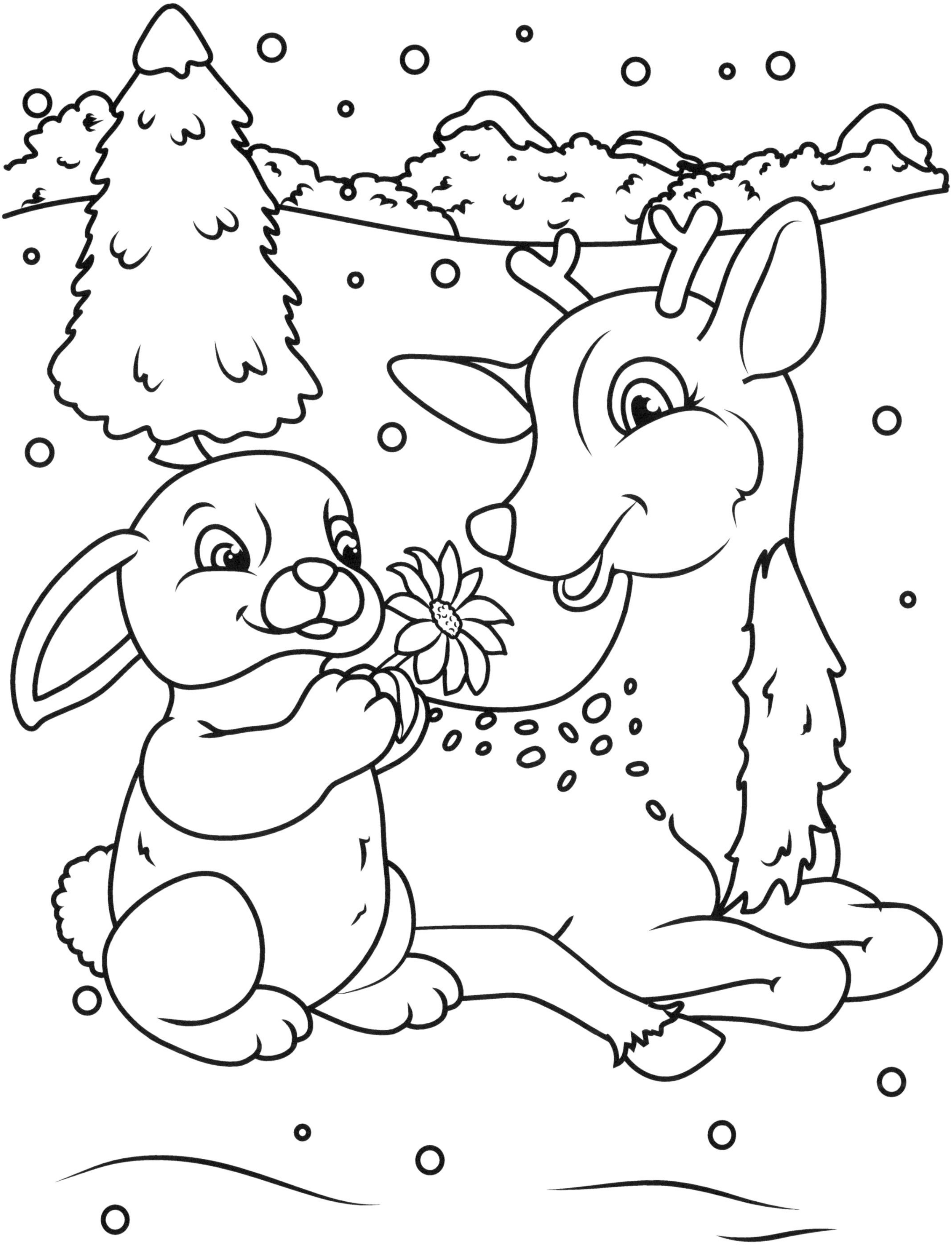

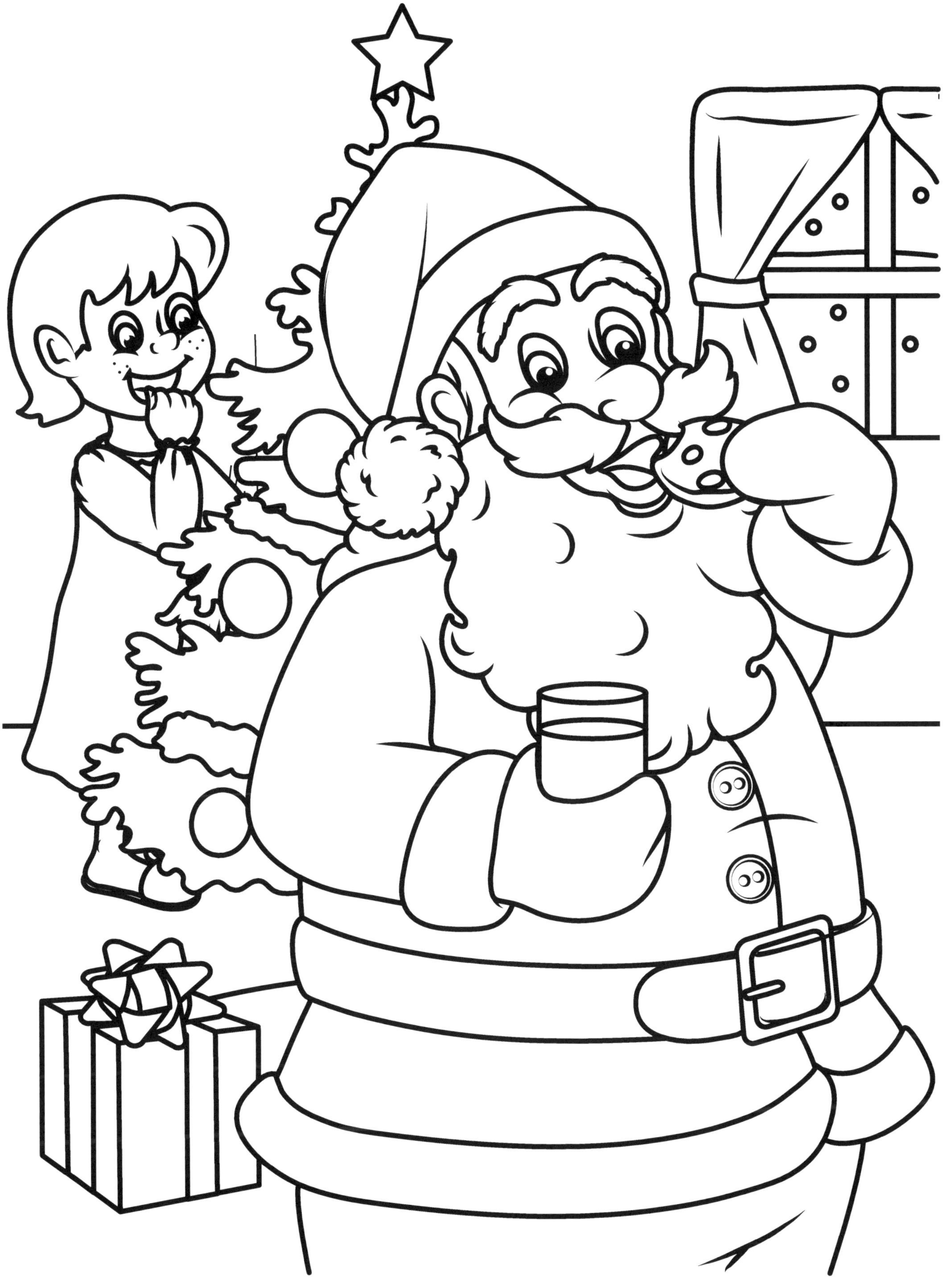

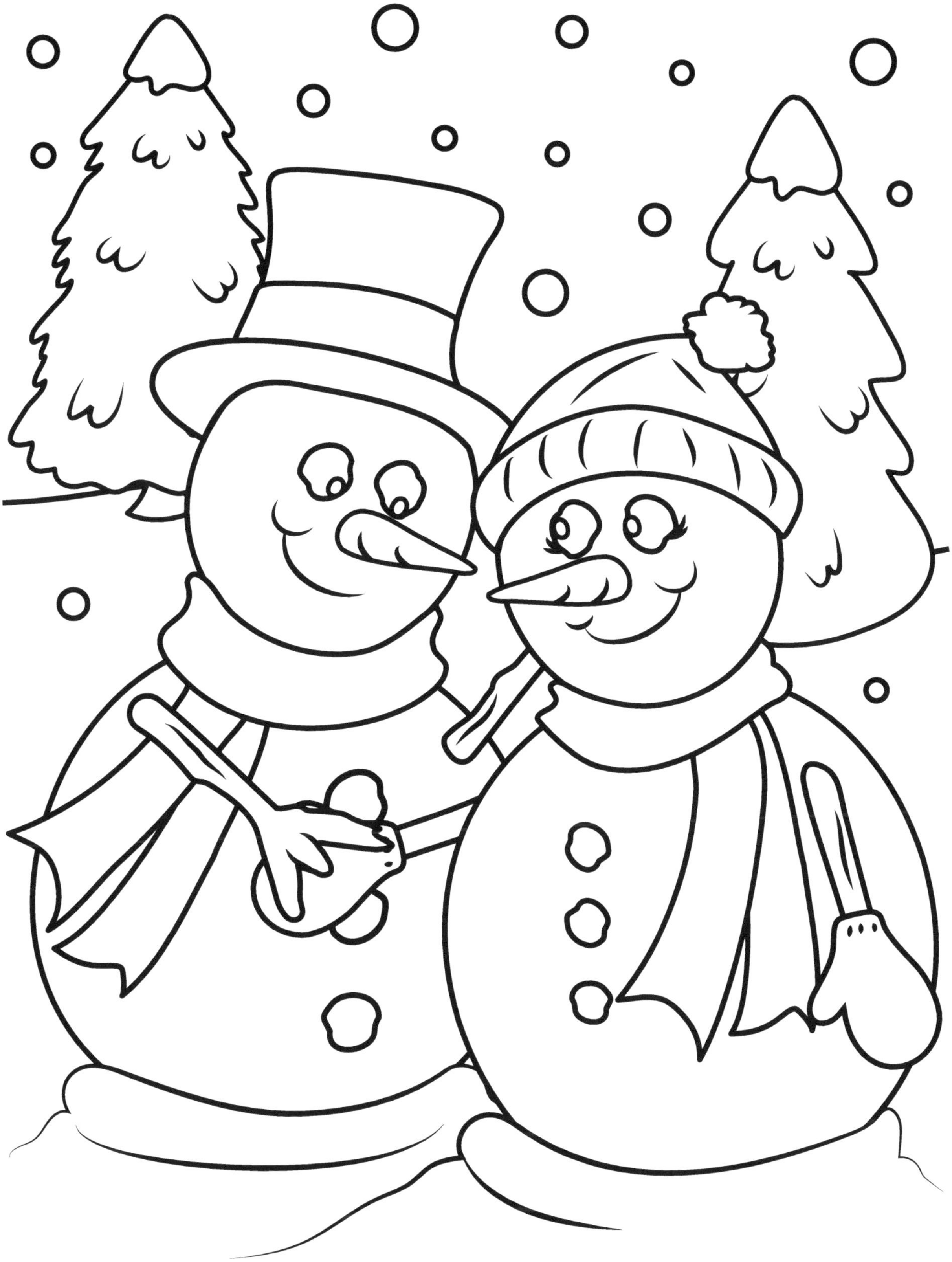

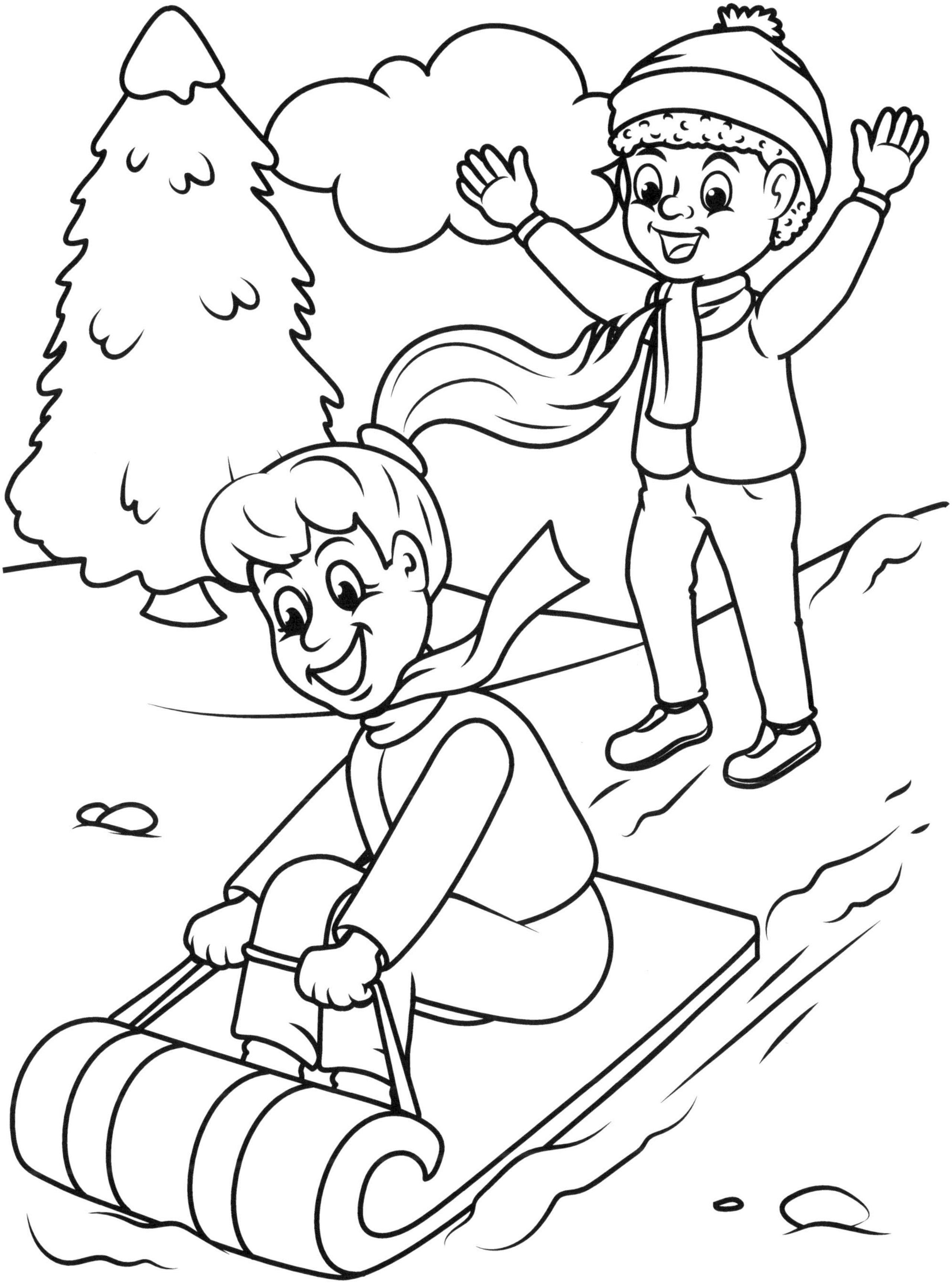

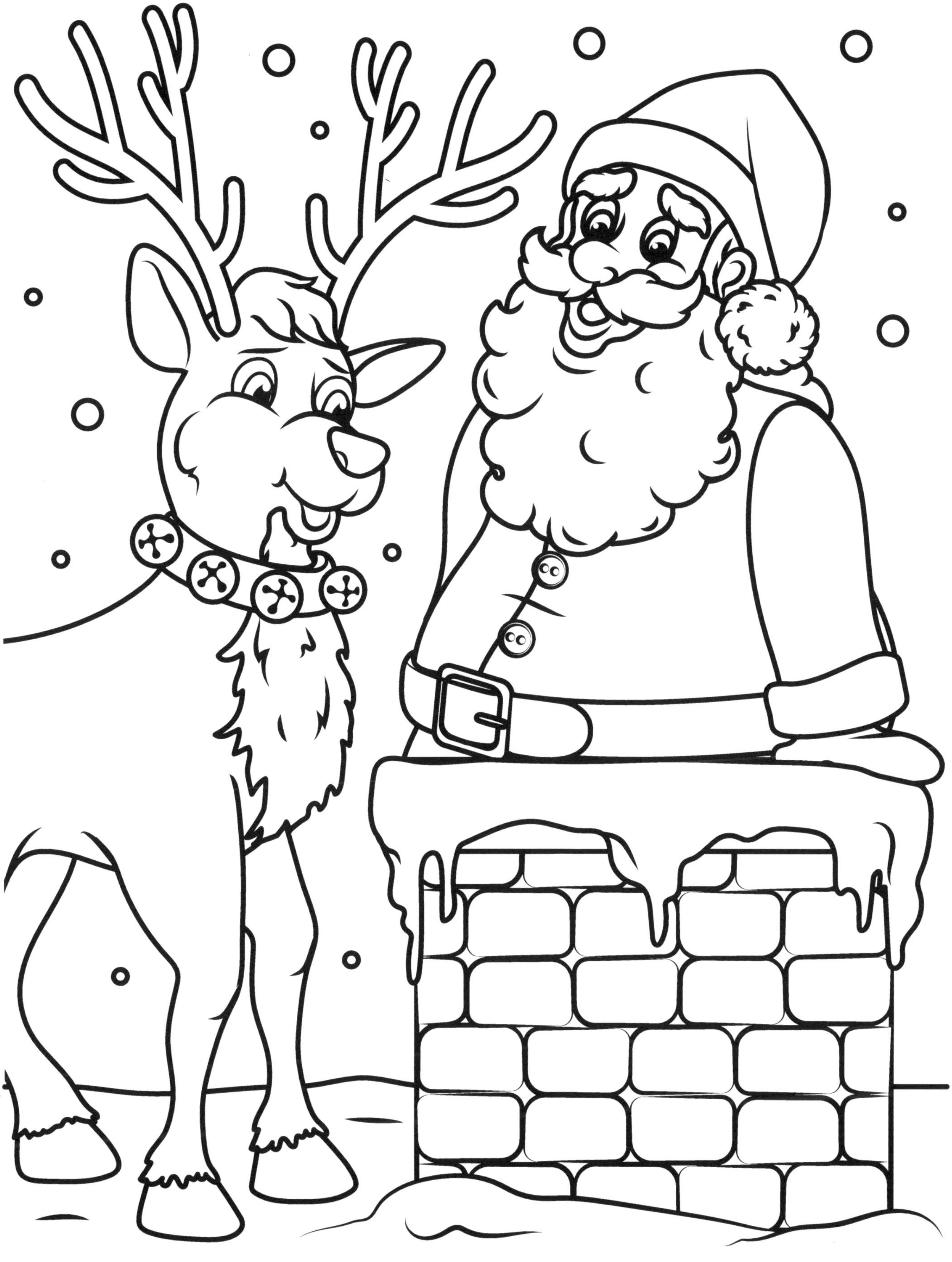

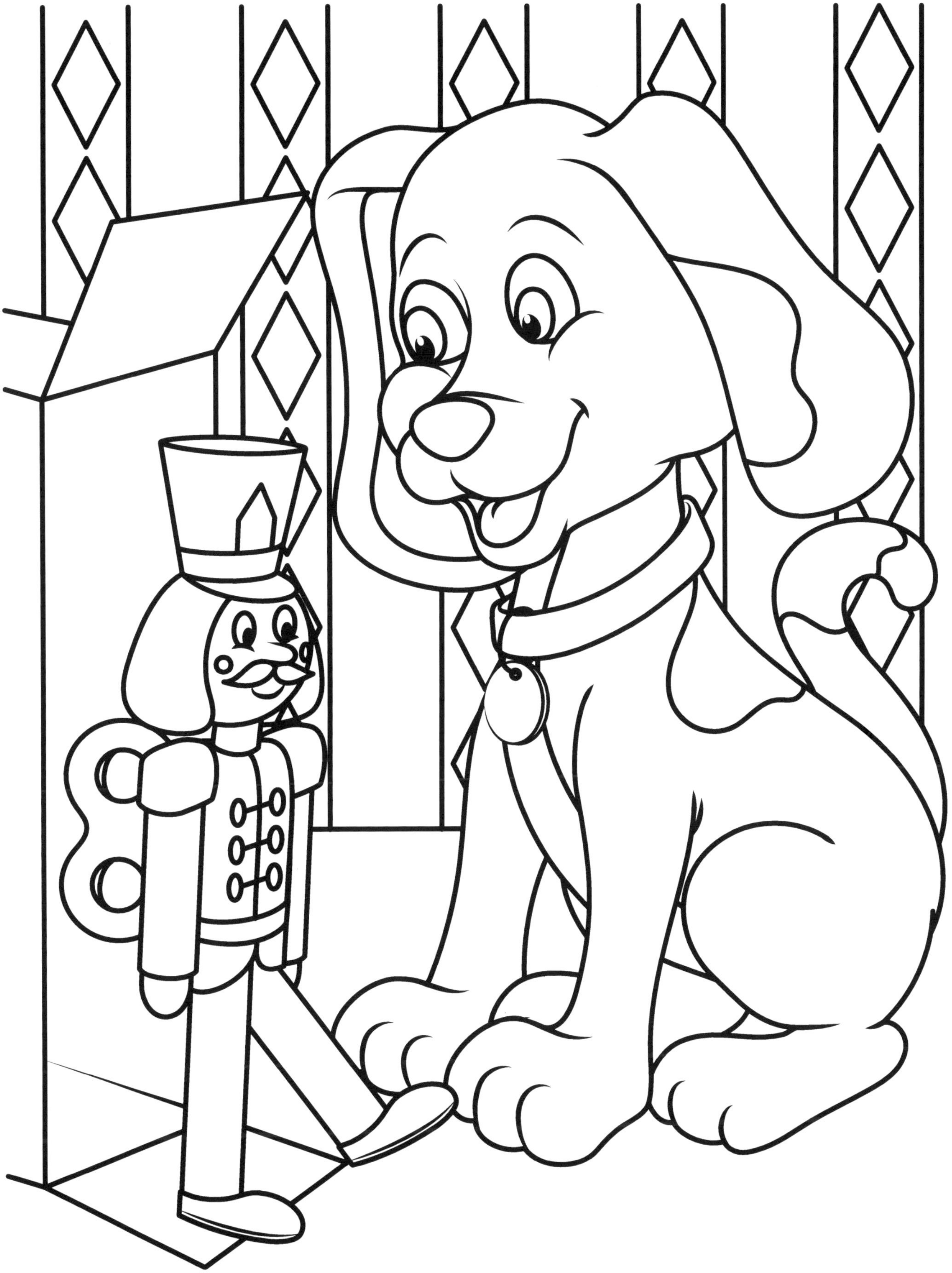

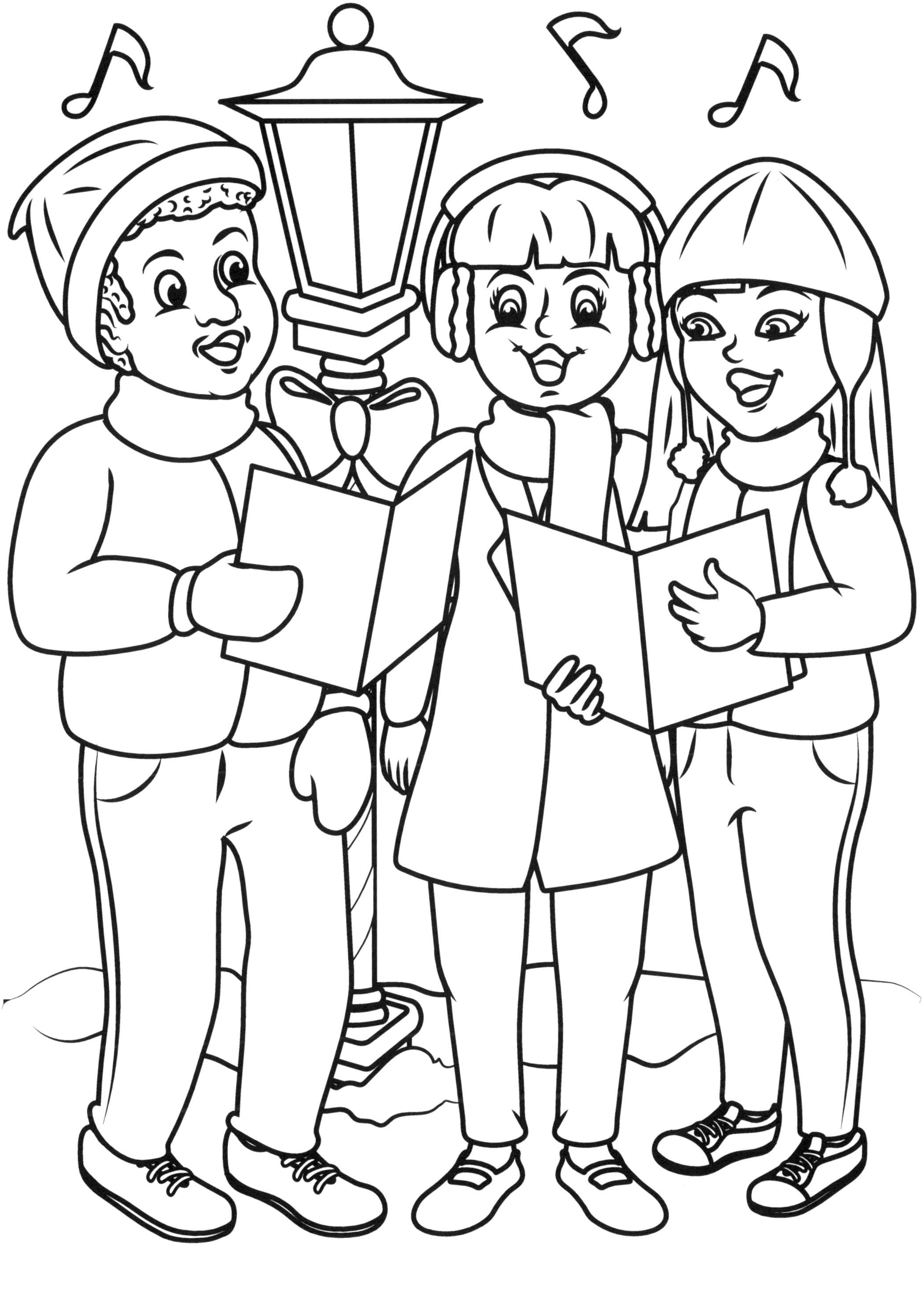

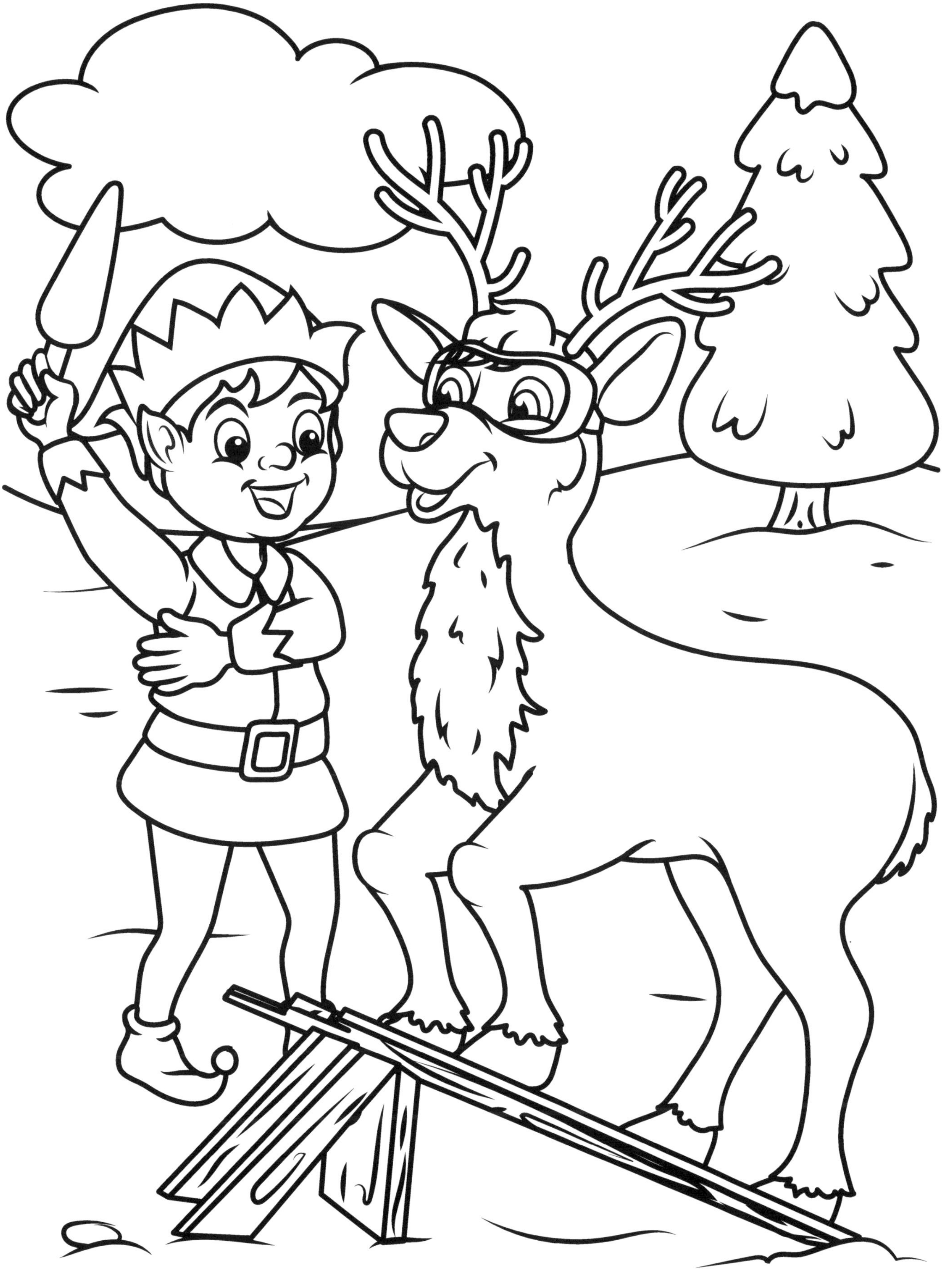

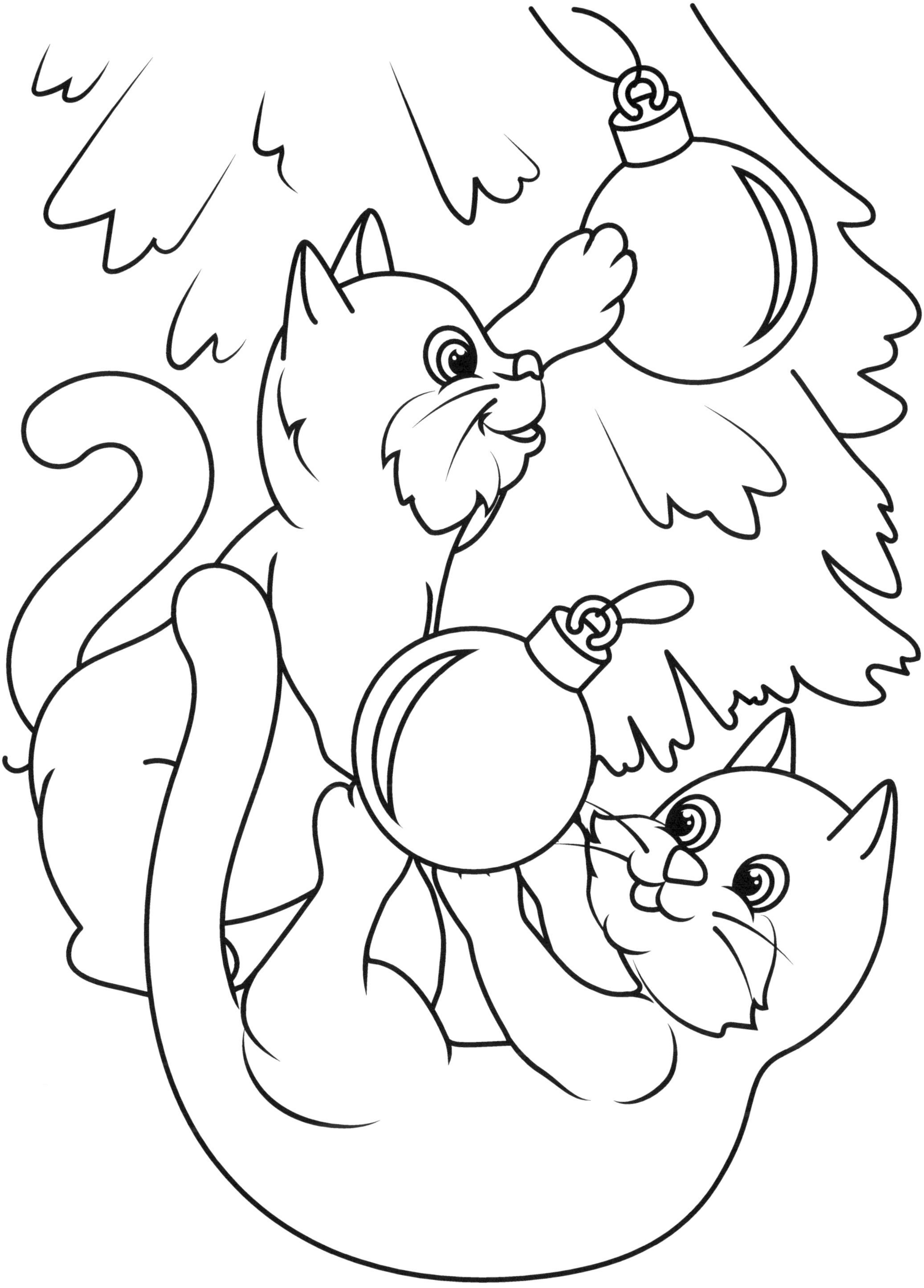

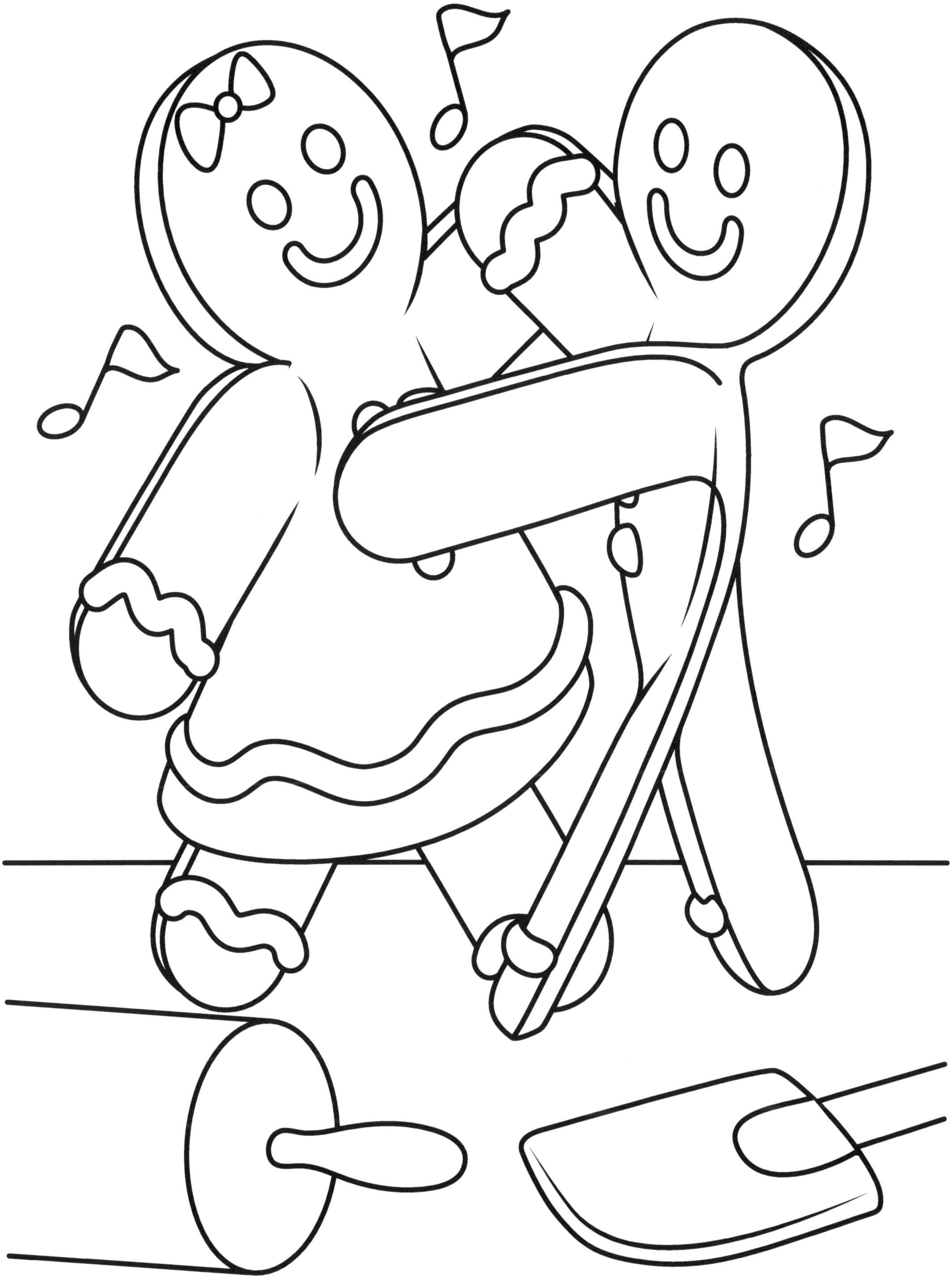

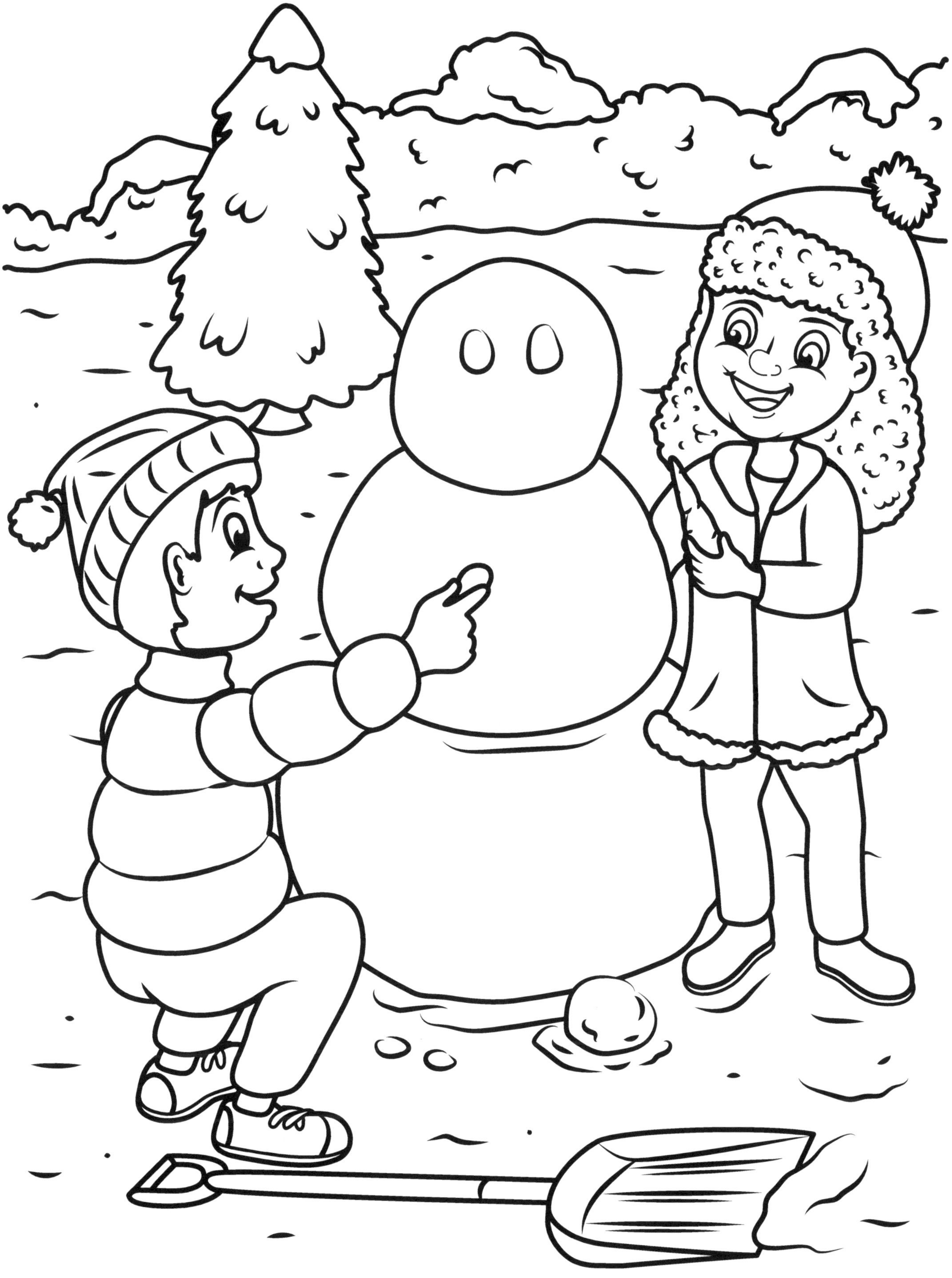

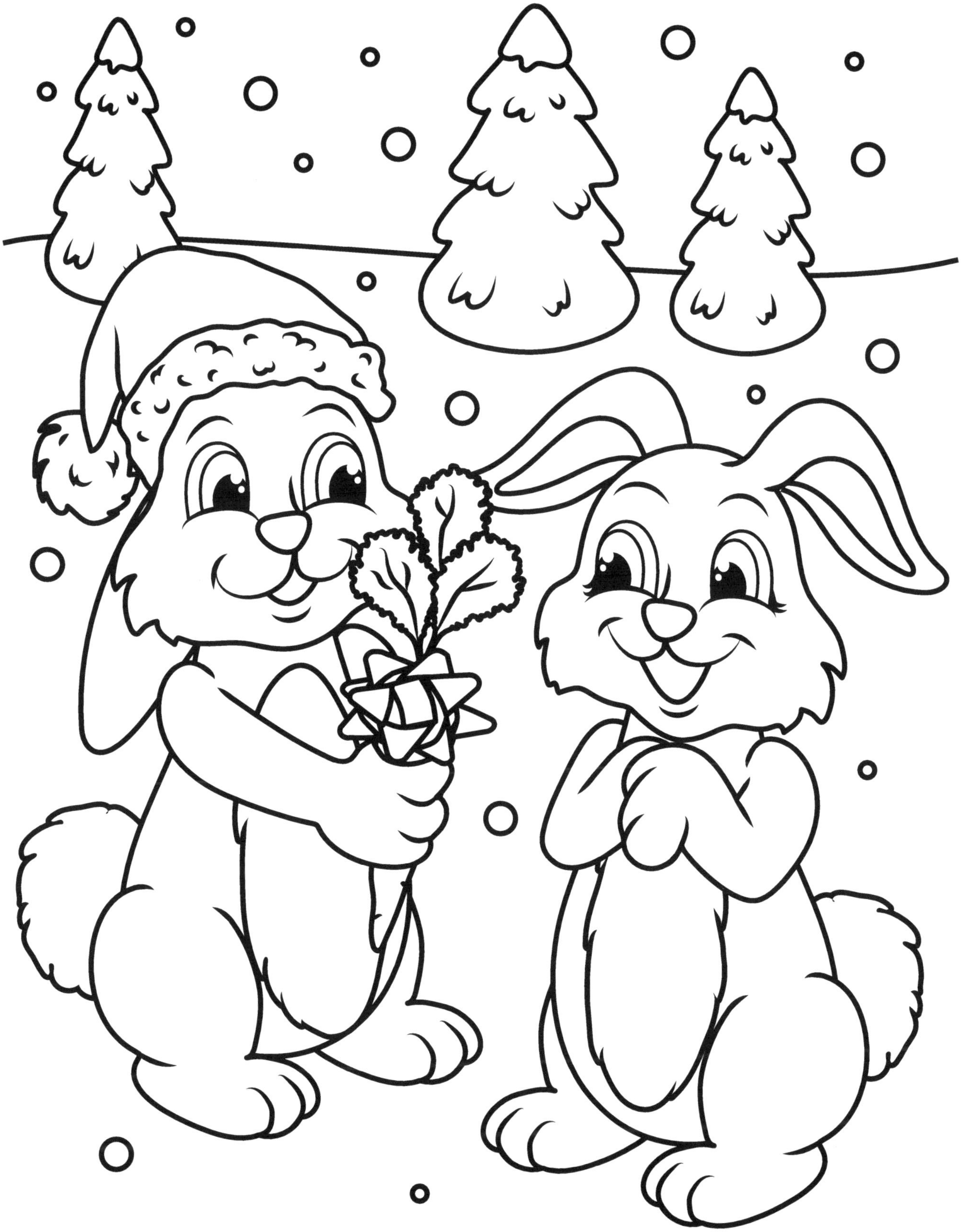

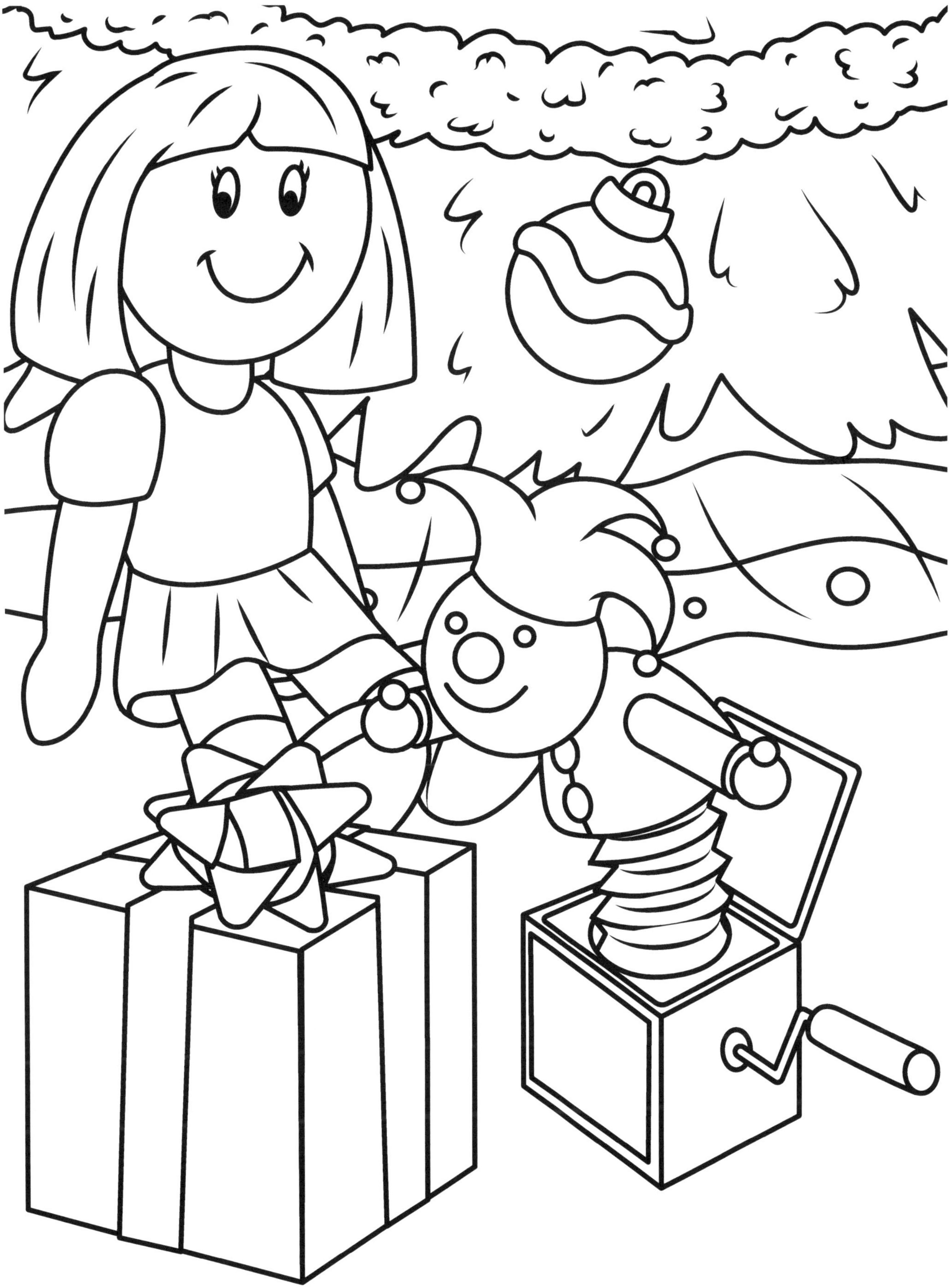

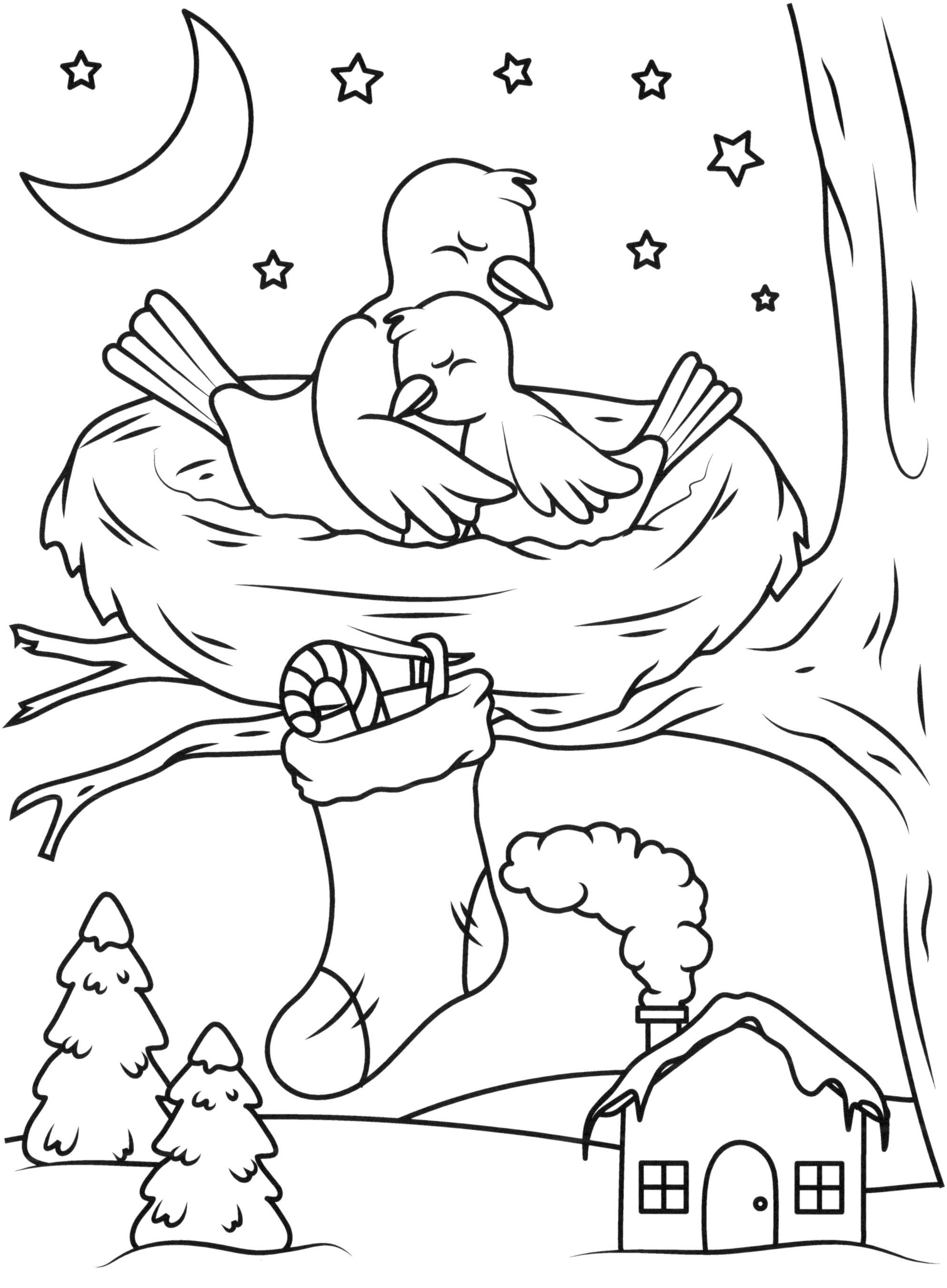

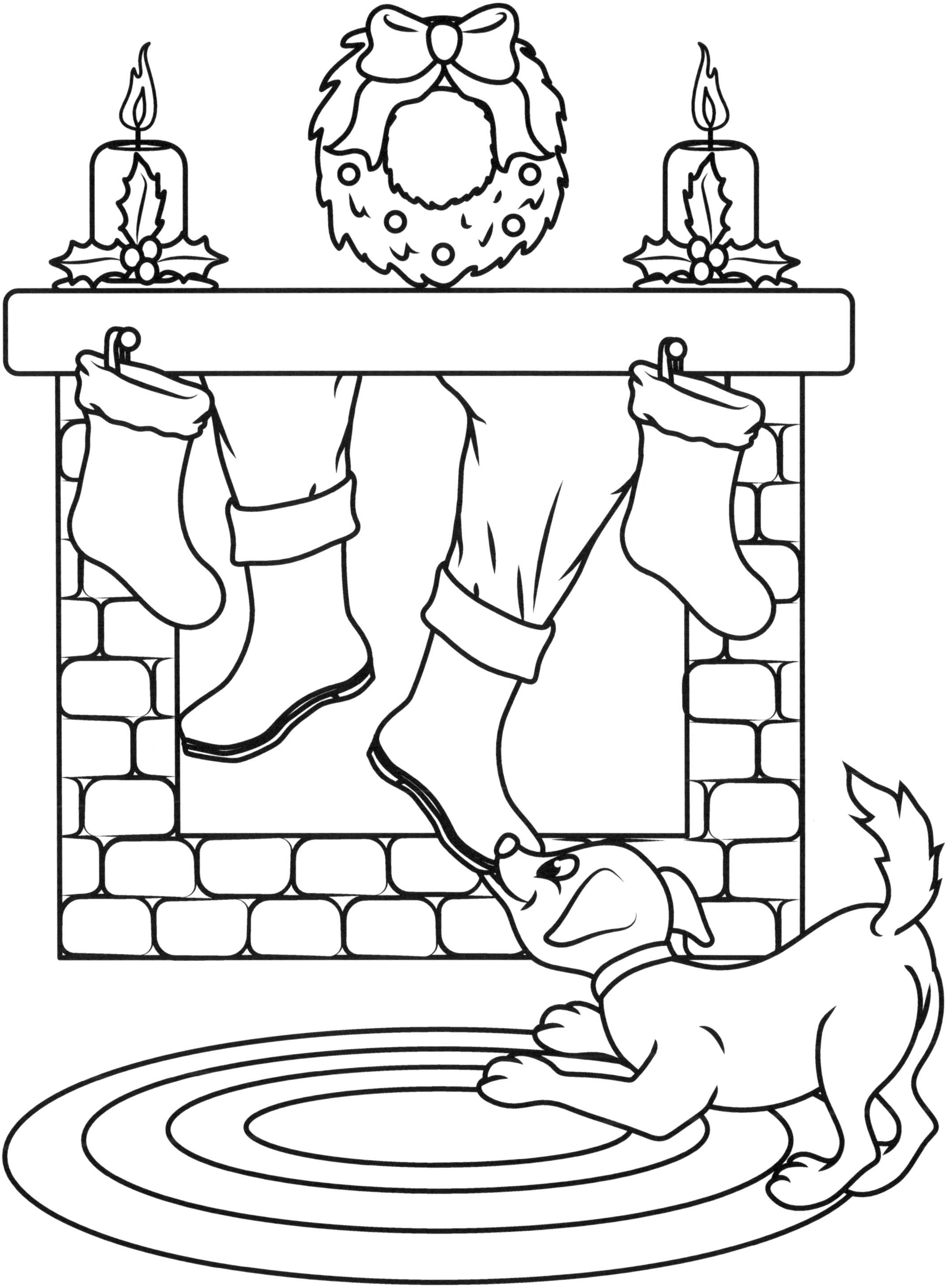

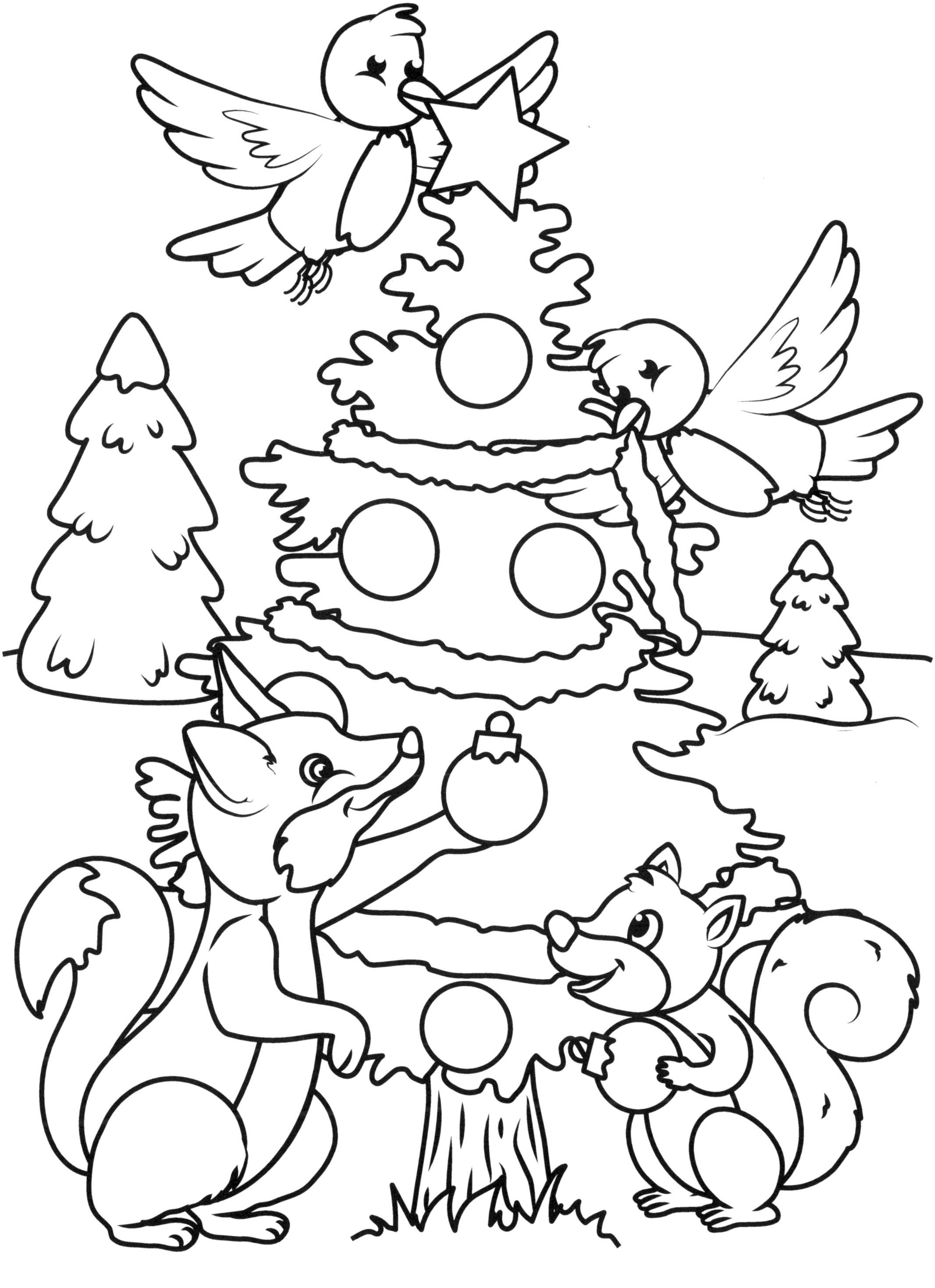

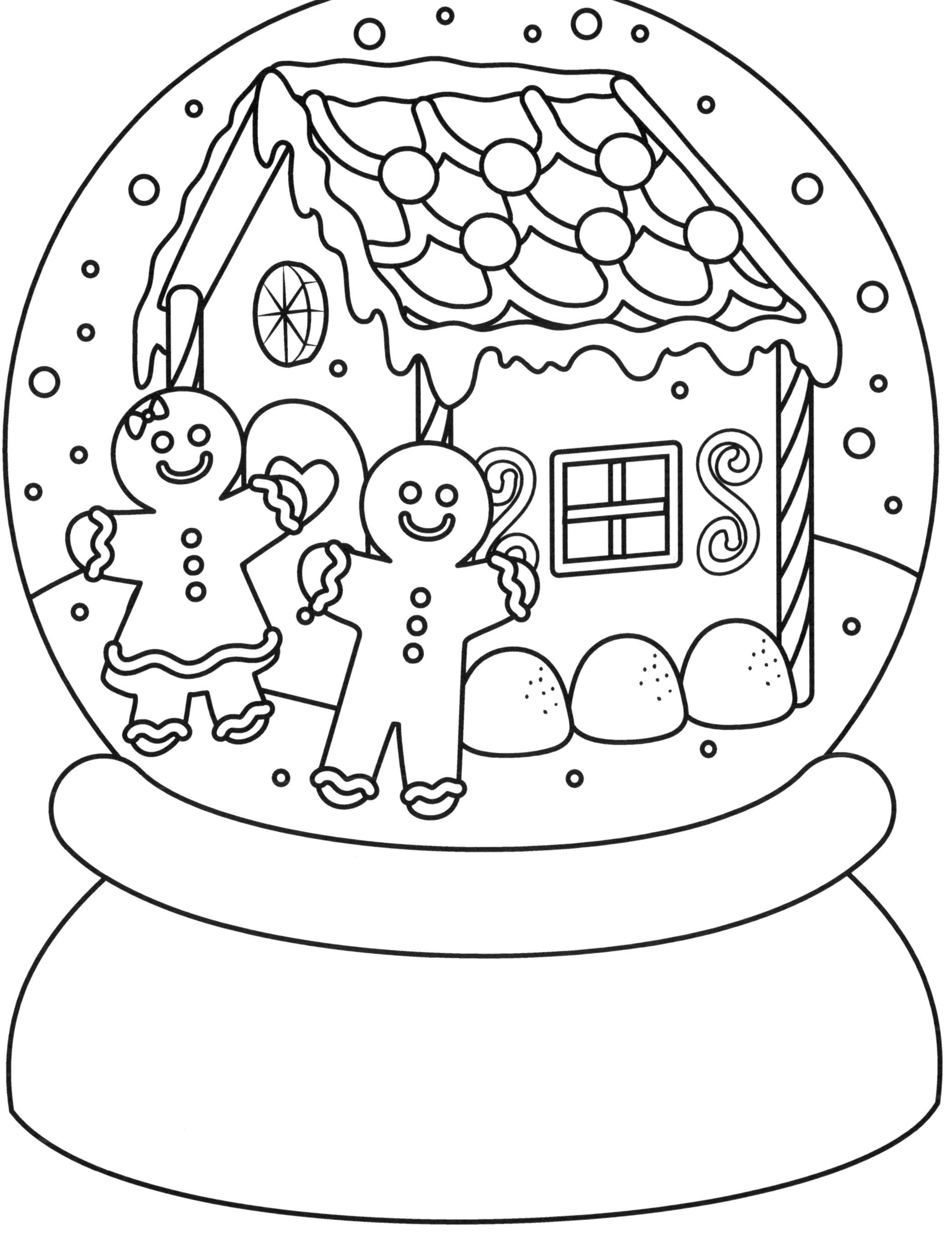

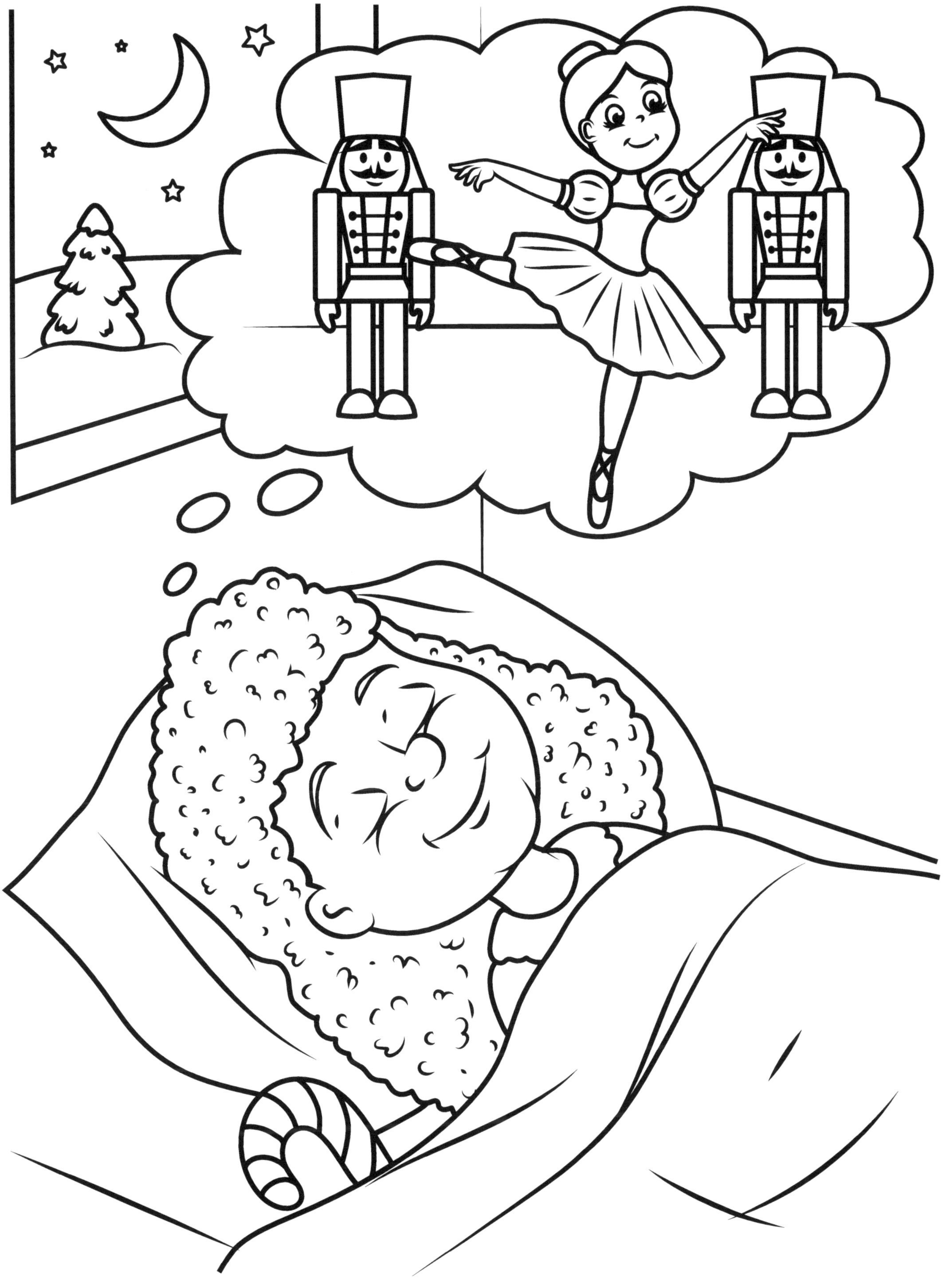

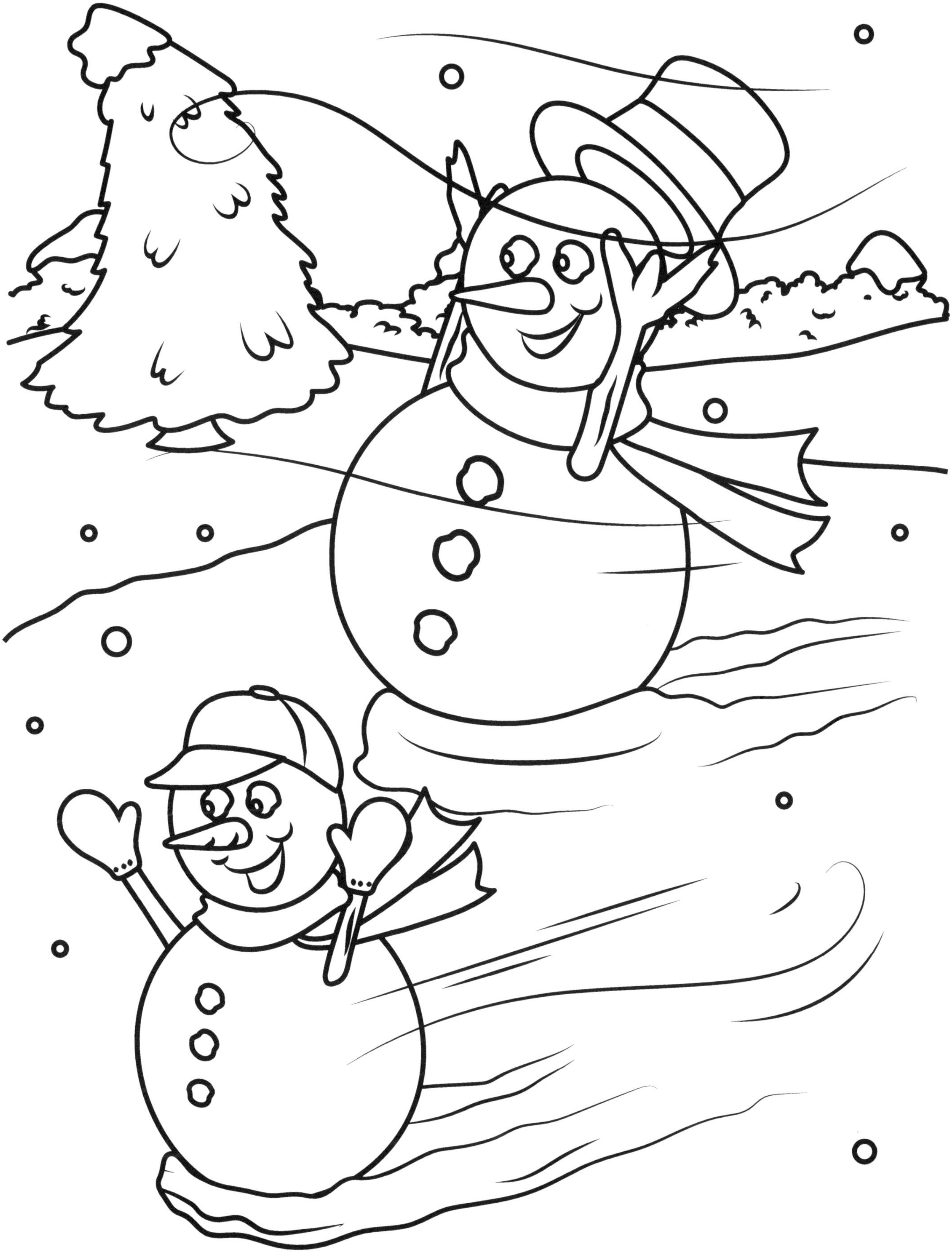

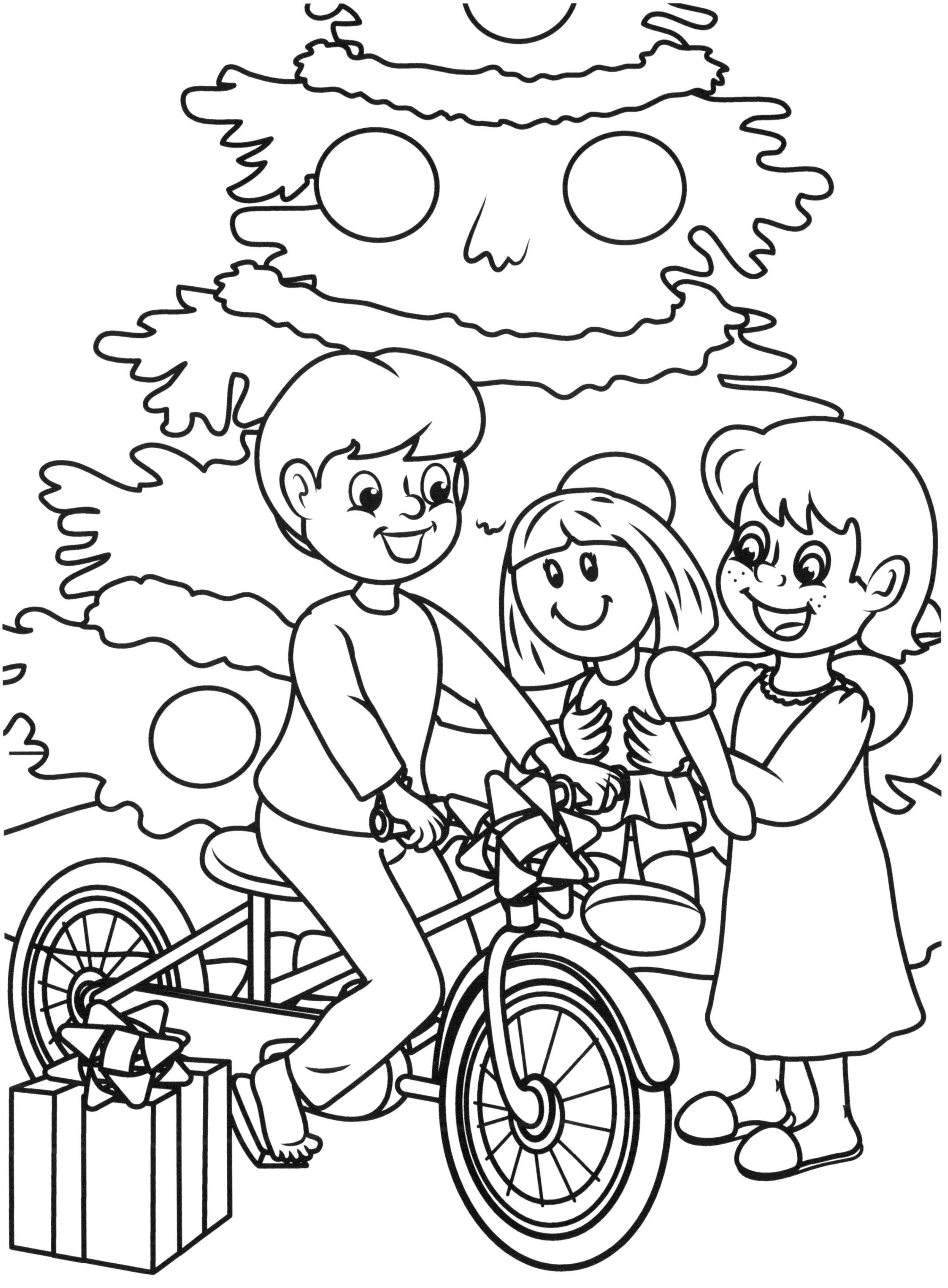

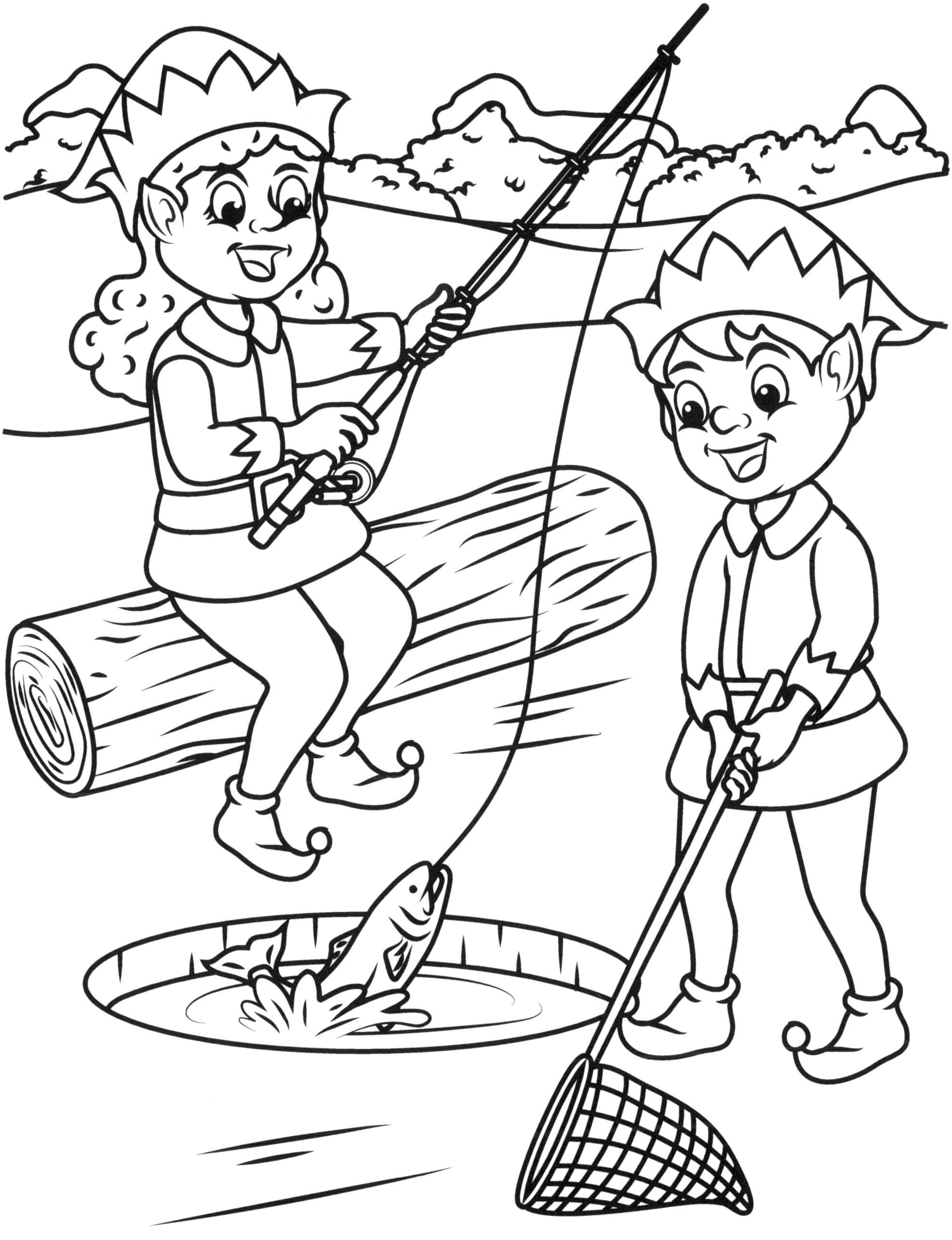

Made in United States
Orlando, FL
12 November 2021

10372988R00035